中国思想文化术语多语种对外翻译
标准化建设项目成果
CHINESE THINKING AND CULTURE
MULTILINGUAL TERMINOLOGY DATABASE

中华源·河南故事
CHINESE CIVILIZATION
Stories from Henan

脱贫攻坚
POVERTY ALLEVIATION

河南省人民政府外事办公室 编

·郑州·

图书在版编目（CIP）数据

中华源·河南故事. 脱贫攻坚：汉、英 / 河南省人民政府外事办公室编. -- 郑州：河南大学出版社，2021.4

ISBN 978-7-5649-4682-1

Ⅰ. ①中… Ⅱ. ①河… Ⅲ. ①地方文化－河南－通俗读物－汉、英②扶贫－概况－河南－汉、英 Ⅳ. ①G127.61-49 ②F127.61

中国版本图书馆CIP数据核字（2021）第084186号

责任编辑	李亚涛
责任校对	林方丽
封面设计	翟淼淼
出版发行	河南大学出版社
	地址：郑州市郑东新区商务外环中华大厦2401号　邮编：450046
	电话：0371-86059701（营销部）
	0371-86059750（高等教育与职业教育分公司）
	网址：hupress.henu.edu.cn
排　版	河南大学出版社设计排版部
印　刷	河南博雅彩印有限公司
版　次	2021年4月第1版
印　次	2021年4月第1次印刷
开　本	710 mm×1010 mm　1/16
印　张	11.75
字　数	194千
定　价	65.00元

版权所有，侵权必究
本书如有印装质量问题，请与河南大学出版社营销部联系调换。

"中华源·河南故事"系列丛书编委会

顾　　问	黄友义　杨　平　范大祺
名誉主任	穆为民　何金平　刘炯天
主　　任	付　静
副 主 任	陈　岩　陈志伟　刁玉华　方启雄　介晓磊
	孔留安　李冰冰　李向前　李　镇　梁留科
	刘金锋　牛卫国　屈鹏飞　史永庆　田　凯
	万正峰　王建修　王清义　王自文　许二平
	杨建伟　杨玮斌　张改平　张俊峰　张明超
	张松文　赵卫东

主　　编	付　静
副 主 编	李冰冰
编　　委	陈　玮　丁　锐　高　阳　徐恒振　郑延保

中华源·河南故事·脱贫攻坚

主　　编	郭奎立
副 主 编	方国根　钱建成（英文）
中文撰稿	宋技明　赵　鹏　梁增辉　范胜利
英文译者	李　洁　贺爱平　张琳琳
英文审校	〔美〕Rex Troumbley

The Editorial Committee
Chinese Civilization
Stories from Henan

Consultants	Huang Youyi Yang Ping Fan Daqi
Honorary Directors	Mu Weimin He Jinping Liu Jiongtian
Director	Fu Jing
Deputy Directors	Chen Yan Chen Zhiwei Diao Yuhua Fang Qixiong
	Jie Xiaolei Kong Liu'an Li Bingbing Li Xiangqian
	Li Zhen Liang Liuke Liu Jinfeng Niu Weiguo
	Qu Pengfei Shi Yongqing Tian Kai Wan Zhengfeng
	Wang Jianxiu Wang Qingyi Wang Ziwen Xu Erping
	Yang Jianwei Yang Weibin Zhang Gaiping
	Zhang Junfeng Zhang Mingchao Zhang Songwen
	Zhao Weidong
Chief Editor	Fu Jing
Deputy Chief Editor	Li Bingbing
Editors	Chen Wei Ding Rui Gao Yang Xu Hengzhen
	Zheng Yanbao

Chinese Civilization
Stories from Henan
Poverty Alleviation

Editor-in-Chief	Guo Kuili
Associate Editors-in-Chief	Fang Guogen Qian Jiancheng (English Text)
Writers	Song Jiming Zhao Peng Liang Zenghui
	Fan Shengli
Translators	Li Jie He Aiping Zhang Linlin
Translation Proofreaders	Rex Troumbley (U.S.)

总　序

中国是世界四大文明古国之一，也是世界上唯一的古代文明传统未曾中断的国家。河南省地处中国中东部，是中华文明和中华民族的重要发祥地，在中国五千年的文明史上，河南作为国家政治、经济、文化的中心就长达三千多年。从某种意义上讲，一部河南史就是半部中国史。这里是中华人文始祖黄帝的故乡，是古丝绸之路的东方起点，是少林功夫和陈氏太极的发源地，这里创建了中国历史上最早的都城，镌刻了中国最古老的文字，诞生了中国最初的商业文明。

伴随着新时代的荣光，河南经济社会发展迅速，人民生活水平显著提升，这是河南人民自力更生、艰苦奋斗的历史结果，也是对外开放带来的益处。河南经济社会的发展、人民生活方式的改变都植根于深层次的文化积淀。为了让世界更多地了解河南，让河南更好地走向世界，2018年以来，河南省人民政府外事办公室认真研析了这片古老土地上的历史文化资源和时代风貌，组织各领域权威专家学者，编译了"中华源·河南故事"中外文系列丛书，选取黄河文化、河洛文化、老子、庄子、黄帝、少林功夫、太极拳、中医、汉字、丝绸之路、古都、农业、大运河、文物、陶瓷、青铜器、手工艺、书法、杂技、豫菜、豫剧、脱贫攻坚、空中丝绸之路、航空城、南水北调、中国粮谷、红旗渠、焦裕禄等多个主题，力图以故事的方式向世界展现一个立体、全面、真实的河南。

当今世界，人类文明无论是在物质还是在精神方面都取得了巨大进步，特别是物质的极大丰富，这在古代世界是完全不能想象的。同时，当代人类也面临着许多突出的难题，比如，贫富差距持续扩大，物欲追求奢华无度，个人主义恶性膨胀，社会诚信不断消减，伦理道德每况愈下，人与自然关系日趋紧张，等等。要解决这些难题，不仅需要运用人类今天的智慧和力量，而且需要运用人类历史上积累和储存的智慧和力量。河南历史文化底蕴深厚、包容性强，在今天仍极具现实意义。中原文化蕴含的思想智慧有助于修身养性，推动人类社会进步发展，焦裕禄精神、红旗渠精神所体现的为民爱民、艰苦奋斗的价值取向是构建人类命运共同体的力量源泉。我们期待与读者们一起从河南故事中汲取更多的智慧和力量，共同创造更加美好的未来。

Series Foreword

China is one of the four ancient civilizations in the world, and is also the only country in the world where the ancient civilization has not been interrupted. Located in east-central China, Henan Province is an important cradle for the Chinese nation and Chinese civilization. In the course of the five thousand years of Chinese history, for more than three thousand years it served as the political, economic and cultural center of the country and therefore, as generally accepted, represents half of the history of China. Henan is the native place of Yellow Emperor, the cradle of Chinese culture, the starting point of the ancient Silk Road in the east, and the birthplace of Shaolin Kungfu and Chen-style Taijiquan—typical examples of the world-renowned Chinese martial arts. It was here that the earliest capital city in China was founded, the oldest Chinese characters engraved, and the earliest commerce took shape.

In the new era, Henan has witnessed rapid growth in its economy and remarkable improvement of people's living conditions owing to the national reform and opening-up policy and unremitting endeavors of the people. Modern economic achievements and social development as well as the changes of way of life could be traced back to its traditional values and cultural heritages. To enable people from other countries to understand Henan, and let the Province integrate more efficiently into the world development, the Foreign Affairs Office of the People's Government of Henan Province has organized teams of authoritative experts and scholars in relevant fields to compile this *Chinese Civilization: Stories from Henan* in Chinese and foreign languages since 2018 by crystallizing the excellence of traditions and outstanding features of modern development. The book series include *The Yellow River Culture*, *Heluo Culture*, *Laozi*, *Zhuangzi*, *The Yellow Emperor*, *Shaolin Kungfu*, *Taijiquan*, *Traditional Chinese Medicine*, *Chinese Characters*, *The Silk Road*, *Ancient Chinese Capitals*, *Feeding the*

People—Agriculture, The Grand Canal, Cultural Heritage, Ceramic, Bronze, Handicraft Art, Calligraphy, Acrobatics, Henan Cuisine, Henan Opera, Poverty Alleviation, Silk Road in the Air, Zhengzhou—An Aviation City, South-to-North Water Diversion, China Grain Valley, Man-Made River—Hongqiqu Canal, A Model Official—Jiao Yulu, etc., presenting a panoramic picture of the Province.

In today's world, human civilization has made great progress in both material accumulation and ethical advancement, and the great abundance of materials today, especially, is beyond the imagination of the ancient people. At the same time, however, modern people are also confronted with a lot of problems, such as the widening gap between the rich and the poor, the indulgence in pursuit of luxury and extravagance, the undesirable extension of individualism, the decline of social integrity, and the increasingly tense relationship between man and nature. To solve the problems, we need to draw on the wisdom and powers developed today as well as those accumulated in the past. Henan is endowed with rich historical and cultural heritages characterized by its inclusiveness, and such heritages remain significant today. The intelligence and wisdom in Henan culture are conducive to self-cultivation and to the promotion of social development. The spirit of serving the people and relentless struggle, as embodied in Jiao Yulu and Man-Made River—Hongqiqu Canal provides source of strength for building a community with a shared future for mankind. It is our hope that wisdom and strength from Henan stories could lead us to a shared brilliant future.

前　言

河南是中华民族的发祥地之一。雄伟的三大山系——太行山、伏牛山、大别山环抱平原，黄河顺滩向东奔流，养育出了远古时期中华民族的最早一批先民。

河南在其独特的自然与历史条件下，长期是中国重要的农业大省和人口大省，但同时也是贫困大省。1978 年时，河南贫困人口有 3687.3 万人，贫困发生率高达 52%。其中，"三山一滩"地区由于自然条件恶劣，集中了河南约 70% 的贫困人口。

新中国成立后，在中国共产党的领导下，河南一直在与贫困做斗争，产生了焦裕禄、杨贵等一批蔑视困难、重整河山的好干部。他们的精神遗产——焦裕禄精神、红旗渠精神，至今仍然是河南乃至全国人民与贫困斗争的精神动力。

中共十八大后，习近平总书记三赴河南视察，做出了一系列重要指示，为打好打赢脱贫攻坚战指明了前进方向。2019 年 9 月，习近平总书记视察河南，首站就深入信阳老区，瞻红察绿，走村入户，看老区新变化，访群众新生活，为新时代老区发展把脉定向、擘画蓝图。

截至 2020 年底，河南省脱贫攻坚战取得了决定性胜利，交上了一份漂亮答卷：53 个贫困县全部脱贫摘帽，9536 个贫困村全部退出贫困序列，718.6 万建档立卡贫困人口脱贫，区域性整体贫困得到基本解决。

在与贫困斗争的历程中，河南人民书写了一个又一个感人至深的脱贫攻坚故事。黄河滩区的兰考自 20 世纪 60 年代初，就有县委书记焦裕禄带领全县人民治理风沙，到 2017 年成为全国第一个脱贫县，已历半个多世纪；伏牛山深处的卢氏县，以金融活水破解了贫困群众产业发展难题；光山县农民从事"多彩田园"生产，到处是"房前屋后一亩茶，一塘肥鱼一群鸭"的场景……一个个动人故事，一项项帮扶政策，一幕幕沧桑变迁，让河南的脱贫攻坚战丰富多彩、荡气回肠。

巍巍高山，汤汤黄河，见证了自古以来河南大地最深刻的一场变化。现在，让这本书带您和我们一起回望脱贫攻坚的历程，倾听筑梦小康的足音。

Preface

Henan Province is one of the birthplaces of Chinese civilization. The three majestic mountains—the Taihang Mountain, the Funiu Mountain and the Dabie Mountain, surround the plain area, and the Yellow River flows eastward, having nurtured the earliest ancestors of the Chinese nation in ancient times.

Henan has long been a major agricultural province with a large population in China. Due to its unique natural and historical conditions, it had been in poverty for a long period of time. In 1978, there were 36.873 million poor people in Henan and the incidence of poverty was as high as 52%. 70% of the poverty-stricken people lived in the "three mountains and one beach area" (the Yellow River beach), where natural conditions were very harsh.

Since the founding of People's Republic of China, Henan has been fighting against poverty under the leadership of the Communist Party of China (CPC), and a group of good officials such as Jiao Yulu and Yang Gui confronted difficulties with great courage. Their spiritual heritages—the spirit of Jiao Yulu and the spirit of the Hongqiqu Canal—are still the spiritual driving force which encourages the people of Henan and all China to struggle against poverty.

After the 18th CPC National Congress, General Secretary Xi Jinping inspected Henan three times and made a series of important instructions, pointing the direction for winning the battle against poverty. In September 2019, during his inspection in Henan, General Secretary Xi went to the old revolutionary base areas of Xinyang first. He walked into the villages, surveyed the changes there, visited local people, and made a blueprint for the development of these areas.

By the end of 2020, Henan Province had won a decisive victory against poverty: 53 counties, 9,536 villages and 7,186 million people had been lifted out of poverty; overall regional poverty had been basically alleviated.

In the course of fighting poverty, the people of Henan Province have shared touching stories of their struggles. In Lankao County of the Yellow River beach area, Jiao Yulu, secretary of the County Party Committee, worked hard with local people to control sandstorms in the early 1960s. More than half a century later, Lankao became the first poverty-free county in China in 2017. Lushi County, located deep in the Funiu Mountain, solved the problem of industrial development for poverty-stricken people with active financial measures. Peasants in Guangshan County are engaged in the project of "colorful countryside," where there are "one *mu* (0.067 hectare) of tea garden, a pond of fish and a flock of ducks around each house." These examples of effective poverty alleviation policies and great changes in people's life make the battle against poverty in Henan Province practical and soul-stirring.

The towering mountains and the rolling Yellow River have witnessed the most profound change in Henan since ancient times. Now, let us look back on the course of our poverty alleviation campaign and listen to the sound of our steps toward a prosperous society.

目 录   Contents

第一章　扶贫道路	001
一、体制改革推动扶贫阶段（1978—1985年）	006
二、大规模开发式扶贫阶段（1986—1993年）	012
三、扶贫攻坚阶段（1994—2000年）	016
四、扶贫开发纲要实施阶段（2001—2012年）	022
五、脱贫攻坚阶段(2013—2020年)	028

Chapter 1　The Path of Poverty Alleviation	001
Ⅰ. Poverty Alleviation through Structural Reform (1978-1985)	007
Ⅱ. Large-scale Development-oriented Poverty Alleviation (1986-1993)	013
Ⅲ. Poverty Alleviation (1994-2000)	017
Ⅳ. Implementation of the Outline of Development-driven Poverty Alleviation (2001-2012)	023
Ⅴ. The Battle against Poverty (2013-2020)	029

第二章　攻坚历程	035
一、坚持一个方略：精准扶贫	036
二、高举一面旗帜：兰考县	044
三、实施十五个专项行动	060

Chapter 2　The Course of Poverty Alleviation	035
Ⅰ. Adhering to One Strategy: Targeted Poverty Alleviation	037
Ⅱ. Holding Up a Banner: Lankao County	045
Ⅲ. Implementing Fifteen Poverty Alleviation Action Plans	061

第三章　全面胜利　151
　　一、聚焦重点难点，攻克最后贫困堡垒　152
　　二、注重作风建设，保障增强扶贫实效　158
　　三、健全长效机制，巩固拓展脱贫成效　162
　　四、做好有效衔接，全面推进乡村振兴　168

Chapter 3　A Sweeping Victory　151
　　Ⅰ. Focusing on Key Problems and Overcoming the Last Bulwark of Poverty　153
　　Ⅱ. Laying Emphasis on Work Style Construction to Ensure More Tangible Results in Poverty Alleviation　159
　　Ⅲ. Improving Long-term Mechanism to Consolidate and Broaden Our Success in Poverty Alleviation　163
　　Ⅳ. Making Effective Connection and Promoting Rural Revitalization in All Respects　169

第一章

扶贫道路

Chapter I

The Path of Poverty Alleviation

河南兰考，一个曾经内涝、风沙、盐碱"三害"肆虐的灾荒之地，因自然条件差，曾是中国知名的贫困县。而贫穷，似乎成了兰考人摆脱不了的标签。

村民游文超祖辈生活在河南省兰考县东坝头乡张庄村。在他的早年人生记忆中，"除了沙，还是沙"。刻在他脑海中的故乡，"人人满面灰土，牙齿一嚼都嘎巴嘎巴响，鼻子经常流血。有时风沙把门堵住了，人只能从窗户爬出去"。

兰考之所以自然环境如此恶劣，是因为地处黄河滩区。黄河作为中国第二大河，它的含沙量在全球范围内都是数一数二的。黄河流域是中华文明的发源地，但它也有一个缺点，即民间所说"三年两决口，百年一改道"。这是指黄河特别容易泛滥，并给沿途带来了风沙灾害。

据《兰考县志》记载，自1644年至中华人民共和国成立的305年间，兰考发生涝灾90多次；自清咸丰至中华人民共和国成立的100多年间，兰考被风沙掩埋的村庄就有63个。1949年，全县97万亩耕地中，低洼易涝地12万多亩，沙碱地33万多亩，全县粮食亩产仅38.5千克。

焦裕禄
Jiao Yulu

Lankao County of Henan Province was once well-known as a poor county in China because it had long been suffering "three natural disasters"—waterlogging, sandstorms, and alkaline soil. Poverty was like a sticky and constantly irritating label attached to the people of Lankao.

You Wenchao's family lived in Zhangzhuang Village, Dongbatou Town of Lankao County for generations. In his earliest memories of Zhangzhuang, You recalls, "There was nothing in the village but dust." In his mind, hometown was a place where "Everyone's face was covered with dust and the teeth rattled when chewing with dust in the mouth. The nose often bled because of the dry weather. Sometimes a sandstorm blocked the door and people had to climb out through the window."

The harsh natural environment of Lankao is related to its geographic location. Lankao is in the beach area of the Yellow River. As the second longest river in China, the Yellow River has the highest sediment concentration in the world. The Yellow River Basin is the birthplace of Chinese civilization, but it also has one drawback. As the folk saying goes, "The Yellow River breached twice in three years, and changed its route once a century." The Yellow River is prone to flooding and brings sandstorm disasters along the way.

According to *The Annals of Lankao County*, during the 305 years from 1644 to the founding of New China, waterlogging occurred more than 90 times. During more than 100 years from the reign of Emperor Xianfeng (the 7th emperor of the Qing Dynasty) to the founding of New China, 63 villages were buried by sandstorms in Lankao. In 1949, among 970,000 *mu* (64,699 hectares) of cultivated land in Lankao, there were 120,000 *mu* (8,004 hectares) of low-lying and waterlogged land, 330,000 *mu* (22,011 hectares) of sandy and alkaline land, and the grain yield per *mu* (0.067 hectare) of the county was only 38.5 kilograms.

In the 1960s, Jiao Yulu, secretary of Lankao County Party Committee, led the people to stabilize the sand and dust through afforestation, grass-planting and sand fixation, and dredging the silt. Although Jiao Yulu worked in Lankao for only 475 days before dying of liver cancer, his painstaking efforts to get rid of poverty have inspired Chinese people generation after generation.

Lankao is a miniature of Henan Province.

At the beginning of New China, Henan was one of the poorest and the most

20世纪60年代，兰考县委书记焦裕禄带领老百姓造林固沙、育草固沙、翻淤压沙。虽然焦裕禄在兰考工作仅475天就因为肝癌而去世，但他为兰考摆脱贫困而付出的心血，感动了几代中国人。

兰考是河南的缩影。

中华人民共和国成立之初，河南是全国最贫困落后的省份之一，人均年工农业总产值为50.3元，比全国平均水平低41%。在1978年改革开放前夕，河南人口约7000万人，有一半处于贫困水平。河南除棉花外，主要农产品人均占有量均低于全国平均水平，处于严重短缺状况，很多地方处于绝对贫困状态。

改革开放40多年来，河南发生了翻天覆地的变化，人民生活水平得到了飞跃式提升。但直到2013年，河南贫困人口仍然不少，总量排全国第3位。

2012年11月中共十八大以来，习近平总书记站在全面建成小康社会、实现中华民族伟大复兴中国梦的战略高度，组织推进了人类历史上规模空前、力度最大、惠及人口最多的脱贫攻坚战。经过8年持续奋斗，中国如期完成了脱贫攻坚目标任务，现行标准下农村贫困人口全部脱贫，贫困县全部摘帽，消除了绝对贫困和区域性整体贫困，9899万贫困人口实现脱贫，取得了令全世界刮目相看的重大胜利。

河南作为中国的农业大省和人口大省，脱贫攻坚同样取得重大胜利。到2020年底，全省实现718.6万建档立卡贫困人口全部脱贫，9536个贫困村全部出列，53个贫困县全部摘帽，消除了绝对贫困和区域性整体贫困。

河南作为中华民族的发源地之一，其近1亿城乡居民在与贫困斗争的过程中，通过一个又一个故事，在历史上留下了值得记忆的痕迹。

backward provinces in the country, with an annual industrial and agricultural output value of 50.3 *yuan* per capita and 41% lower than the national average. On the eve of the reform and opening-up in 1978, half of Henan's 70 million people lived in poverty. Except for cotton, the per capita share of main agricultural products in Henan was lower than the national average level and was in a serious shortage. Many places in Henan were in absolute poverty.

Over the past 40 years of reform and opening-up, great changes have taken place in Henan and people's living standard has been improved by leaps and bounds. However, until 2013, the number of the poor population in Henan was still large and ranked third in China.

After the 18th CPC National Congress in November 2012, General Secretary Xi Jinping put forward the strategy of building a moderately prosperous society in all respects and realizing the great dream of China's rejuvenation. Xi staged a battle against poverty that is unprecedented in scale and intensity and has benefited the largest number of people in human history. Through 8 years of continuous struggle, China has completed the target task of poverty alleviation. According to China's current poverty line, all impoverished rural residents have been lifted out of poverty, all impoverished counties have been removed from the poverty list, absolute poverty and regional overall poverty have been eliminated, and 98.99 million poor people have been lifted out of poverty. A great victory against poverty has been achieved and China has earned the admiration of the world.

As a large agricultural province with a large population, Henan has also won the battle against poverty. By the end of 2020, 7.186 million registered poor people had been lifted out of poverty, 9,536 villages had risen high enough to be removed from the poverty list, 53 poor counties had been lifted out of poverty, and absolute poverty and regional overall poverty had been eliminated.

Henan is one of the birthplaces of the Chinese nation. Nearly 100 million urban and rural residents in Henan had struggled against poverty. They left behind heartbreaking stories of Henan's struggle with poverty that can never be forgotten.

一、体制改革推动扶贫阶段（1978—1985年）

1978年，中共十一届三中全会开启了农村改革的新进程。

1982年1月1日，中共中央发出第一个"一号文件"，正式承认农村家庭联产承包责任制。"包产到户"从根本上打破了农业生产经营和分配的"大锅饭"，使农民有了真正的自主权。这种"交足国家的，留够集体的，剩下都是自己的"经营模式，利益关系简单明了。当农民分到了自己的责任田的时候，生产积极性大为高涨。

"大包干"使得河南省的粮食产量实现了第一个大的飞跃。1983年，《河南日报》曾经报道了发生在兰考县城关镇刘廷贺家的巨大变化。1978年前，全家人经常为吃不饱饭发愁，实行"大包干"后，全家人起早贪黑，精心管理责任田，到1982年，全家10口人人均占有粮食1100千克，人均收入现金1200元。

改革开放后的前几年，河南省粮食产量以惊人的速度迅速拉升。统计数据表明，全省粮食产量由1978年的2097万吨增加到1983年的3303万吨，人均粮食占有量由1978年的148.5千克迅速增加到1983年的383.5千克，增长了158%。1983年，全省不仅历史性地完全解决了省内居民的温饱问题，并且开始成为粮食调出省。

与此同时，河南的农村扶贫工作作为社会救济的一部分，1979年开始试点，1980年铺开。扶持的对象最初为因主要劳力死亡、残疾、长期患病或遭受意外不幸事故，以及人口多、劳力少等原因造成生活困难的严重困难户、贫困户，1984年又增加烈、军属，复员、退伍军人等优抚对象（简称"双扶"）。扶贫工作的区域重点放在老革命根据地、山区、老灾区和历史贫困地区。1984年省政府成立河南省革命老根据地建设领导小组，确定对大别山、桐柏山区的新县、商城、光山、固始、罗山、潢川、信阳、桐柏、确山9个县中的老区乡、村进行重点扶持。

I. Poverty Alleviation through Structural Reform (1978-1985)

In 1978, the Third Plenary Session of the 11th CPC Central Committee launched a new process of rural reform.

On January 1, 1982, the CPC Central Committee issued the first "No.1 Document" to formally recognize the rural household contract responsibility system, which fundamentally broke the "big pot" of agricultural production and distribution, giving peasants real autonomy. This kind of production model clarifies the relationship among the country, the collectives and the peasants vividly, "After making enough contribution to the country and the collectives, the rest are their own." When the peasants were assigned responsibility fields, their enthusiasm for production was greatly aroused.

The "contract responsibility system" stimulated the first big leap of grain yield in Henan Province. In 1983, *Henan Daily* reported the great changes that took place for Henan's people. Liu Tinghe's family in Chengguan Town of Lankao County is one vivid example. Before 1978, the family often worried about hunger. After the implementation of the "contract responsibility system," the family worked hard in their fields day and night. In 1982, this family of ten had 1,100 kilograms of grain and 1,200 *yuan* per capita.

In the first few years of reform and opening-up, grain yield of Henan Province increased at an amazing rate. Statistics show that the grain yield of the whole province increased from 20.97 million tons in 1978 to 33.03 million tons in 1983, and the per capita share of grain increased rapidly from 148.5 kilograms in 1978 to 383.5 kilograms in 1983, an increase of 158%. In 1983, Henan Province could not only assure that people had adequate food and clothing, but also began sending surplus grains to other places.

At the same time, the rural poverty alleviation work in Henan Province started in 1979 as a part of social relief, and it was promoted in a large scale from 1980. At first, relief targets were the families with severe difficulties and poverty due to the death, disability, and long-term illness or accidents of the family bread

1985年省委、省政府成立了河南省山区建设领导小组,做出《关于帮助山区和贫困地区尽快改变面貌的决定》,确定对25个重点山区县和22个有部分山区乡的县,进一步放宽政策,改善生产条件,进行扶持。

随着人民生活水平的快速改善,"万元户"一词在20世纪80年代初出现了,这是指那些存款或者收入在1万元以上的家庭。1985年人民币汇率是1美元兑2.9元人民币,1万人民币差不多能兑换3448美元。在当时,"万元户"是那些脱离了贫困、"先富起来"的富裕群体的标签。

改革开放初期,信阳市固始县农民蔡林义敢想敢干,受一部分人先富起来思想的影响,1981年靠着卖粮的收入,在房前屋后、责任田四周种了4000多棵树苗发展林业种植,又承包鱼塘养鱼,养殖猪、牛、羊、鹅。另外,他还把家庭的生意扩展到磨粉、打油、做挂面、做豆腐。在蔡林义的带领下,蔡家在联产承包责任制刚推行一年后,收入就超过了万元,并被河南省政府表彰,成为河南首个经官方认可的"万元户"。

这一阶段,河南省在农村经济体制改革的推动下,全省贫困人口急剧减少。截至1985年底,基本脱贫46万多户,占贫困户总数的48%。按照1985年国家统计局根据全国农村住户调查数据、运用"热量—恩格尔系数法"测算得到的农民人均年纯收入206元的贫困标准,河南省农村贫困人口由1978年的2500万人减少到1985年的1350万人。

earners, as well as the impoverished families with more members but insufficient working capacity. In 1984, dependents of martyrs, military families, demobilized soldiers, and veterans became targets of preferential care (referred to as "double support"). The regional focus of poverty alleviation was the old revolutionary base areas, mountainous areas, old disaster areas, and historically poverty-stricken areas of Henan. In 1984, Henan provincial government set up a leading group for the construction of the old revolutionary base areas, which decided to give key support to the old towns and villages in the nine counties of the Dabie Mountain and the Tongbai Mountain, including Xinxian, Shangcheng, Guangshan, Gushi, Luoshan, Huangchuan, Xinyang, Tongbai and Queshan. In 1985, Henan provincial Party committee and the government set up a leading group for the construction of mountainous areas, which issued *Decisions on Aiding Mountainous Areas and Poverty-stricken Areas to Change Their Conditions Quickly*, and decided to support 25 key mountainous counties and 22 counties with some mountainous towns by providing more favorable policies and improving production conditions.

With the rapid improvement of people's lives, the term "households with 10,000 *yuan*" appeared in the early 1980s to refer to families that had risen from poverty earlier than others with incomes or savings of more than 10,000 *yuan*. In 1985, the exchange rate between RMB and U.S. dollar was 2.9 to 1, and 10,000 *yuan* could be converted to 3,448 U.S. dollars.

In the early days of the reform and opening-up, Cai Linyi, a peasant in Gushi County of Xinyang City, was bold in thinking and doing. In 1981, Cai was encouraged by the idea that "some people could get rich first." With the income earned from selling grains, he bought more than 4,000 saplings and planted them around his house and fields to develop forestry cultivation. He also constructed fish ponds and raised pigs, cattle, sheep, and geese. Cai expanded his business to flour milling, oil refining, and dried noodle and tofu production. Under the leadership of Cai Linyi, his family earned more than 10,000 *yuan* just one year after the implementation of the "contract responsibility system," and was commended by Henan provincial government, becoming the first officially recognized "household with 10,000 *yuan*" in Henan.

During this period of reform for the rural economic system, the poor population in Henan Province decreased sharply. By the end of 1985, more than

山区带贫产业——盛开的油菜花（摄影：唐笑）
Poverty alleviation project in the mountainous areas—fields of blooming canola flowers
(Photographer: Tang Xiao)

460,000 households had been lifted out of poverty, accounting for 48% of the total number of previously poverty-stricken households. According to the poverty line of per capita annual net income of 206 *yuan* calculated by the National Bureau of Statistics in 1985 following the national rural household survey data and "calorie—Engel coefficient," the number of the rural residents fell in Henan Province from 25 million in 1978 to 13.5 million in 1985.

二、大规模开发式扶贫阶段（1986—1993 年）

20 世纪 80 年代中期，河南省农村贫困问题得到明显缓解，贫困人口大幅减少，但是一些自然条件较差、生态环境恶化、经济发展水平较低地区的贫困问题凸显出来。

1986 年，国务院成立贫困地区经济开发领导小组，开始大规模的扶贫开发工作。河南省也将省老区建设领导小组和省山区建设领导小组合并，成立省贫困地区领导小组，下设办公室，负责全省老革命根据地、山区和多灾贫困地区的扶贫开发工作，并于当年确定 22 个贫困县。后来经多次调整，到 1989 年时，全省贫困县定为 30 个，照顾县定为 4 个，共计 34 个县。

1990 年 3 月，河南省政府就开发建设山区制定了一系列政策措施。省委、省政府积极开展科技扶贫，先后为 34 个贫困县和贫困照顾县选派了科技副县长，鼓励科技人员下乡、下厂为贫困地区经济开发做贡献。1991 年，重点开展对口扶贫工作，协调组织 40 个省直单位对口扶持 34 个贫困县，签订扶贫目标责任书，完不成任务不得脱钩。1992 年编制实施《河南省贫困地区"八五"支柱产业发展规划》，在贫困地区因地制宜地开发、建立了各具特色的商品生产基地。

20 世纪 80 年代，地处深山的西峡县曾经是河南的贫困山区县之一。为摆脱贫困，西峡县抓住"南菇北移"机会，大力培育香菇产业。从 1982 年到 1997 年，西峡县成为全国最大的椴木香菇生产基地，当时菇农多达 5 万户、近 20 万人。到 2020 年，西峡已经成为全国最大的香菇交易市场，该市场所在的双龙镇双龙村，人口仅千余人，但香菇交易门店多达 400 家，常驻外地客商 300 余人，常年从事香菇加工、分级、购销的人员 5000 余人，市场年交易干菇 360 万千克，交易额超过 14 亿元，整个西峡县香菇年交易额超过 200 亿元，平均每 10 个西峡人中就有 6

II. Large-scale Development-oriented Poverty Alleviation (1986-1993)

In the mid-1980s, rural poverty in Henan Province was substantially alleviated and the number of poor people dropped significantly. However, poverty problems in some areas caused by unfavorable natural conditions, deteriorating ecological environment, and a low level of economic development were prominent.

In 1986, the State Council set up a leading group for economic development in poverty-stricken areas to launch large-scale poverty alleviation and development programs. Henan Province combined the provincial leading group for the construction of the old revolutionary base areas with the leading group for the construction of the mountainous areas and established the provincial leading group for poverty-stricken areas, which was responsible for poverty alleviation and development in the old revolutionary base areas, mountainous areas, and disaster-prone poor areas of Henan. 22 poor counties were identified that year. By 1989, there had been 30 registered poor counties and 4 counties under poverty assistance, 34 in total.

In March 1990, Henan provincial government formulated a series of policies and measures on the development and construction of the mountainous areas. The provincial Party committee and the government carried out poverty alleviation actively through science and technology. They selected and appointed deputy heads responsible for the development of science and technology for the above-mentioned 34 counties, and encouraged scientific and technological personnel to relocate to the countryside and factories where they could best contribute to the economic development of the poverty-stricken areas. In 1991, Henan provincial government focused on paired-up assistance of poverty alleviation, coordinated, and organized 40 government-affiliated institutions to assist the 34 poor counties. They signed the letter of responsibility for poverty alleviation target, and could not decouple without completing the target. In 1992, *The 8th Five-Year Plan for the Development of Pillar Industries in Poor Areas of Henan Province* was formulated and implemented, and commodity production bases of various characteristics were

人从事着与香菇有关的工作。

　　各种开发式扶贫政策和措施实施力度的加大，对全省加快扶贫进程起到了巨大推动作用。全省农村贫困人口从1985年的1350万人减少到1993年的760万人，占农村人口总数的比重下降到10%。

developed and established in these areas according to local conditions.

In the 1980s, Xixia County was one of the poor mountainous counties in Henan Province. In order to get rid of poverty, the county seized the opportunity of "moving mushrooms from South to North" (the strategy proposed by China's edible fungi industry in 1994) and vigorously developed mushroom cultivation. From 1982 to 1997, Xixia became the largest basswood mushroom production site in China, with 50,000 households and nearly 200,000 people participating in mushroom production at that time. By 2020, Xixia had had the largest lentinus edodes trading market in China. Shuanglong Village of Shuanglong Town, where the market is located, has a population of only 1,000 people. However, there are as many as 400 stores dealing in lentinus edodes; more than 300 merchants from other places, and more than 5,000 people are engaged in processing, grading, purchasing and marketing of lentinus edodes all through the year. The market trades 3.6 million kilograms of dried mushrooms annually, with a trading volume of over 1.4 billion *yuan*. The annual trading volume of Xixia County as a whole is over 20 billion *yuan* and every 6 out of 10 people in Xixia are engaged in mushroom industry.

The intensive implementation of various development-oriented poverty alleviation policies and measures has accelerated the process of poverty alleviation in Henan Province. The number of rural poor people in the province decreased from 13.5 million in 1985 to 7.6 million in 1993, accounting for 10% of the total rural population.

三、扶贫攻坚阶段（1994—2000年）

1994年，国务院出台《国家八七扶贫攻坚计划》，决定集中人力、物力和财力，用7年左右的时间，到2000年底基本解决8000万农村贫困人口的温饱问题。当时，河南有28个县列入国家"八七扶贫攻坚计划"重点扶持县，6个县被列为省重点扶持县。

河南省委、省政府为落实党中央、国务院的战略决策，制定扶贫攻坚计划，1994年4月，省委、省政府召开全省扶贫开发暨农村工作会议，决定到20世纪末，基本解决全省760万贫困人口的温饱问题；同年5月，省政府制定《河南省1994—2000年扶贫攻坚计划》；同年6月，省委、省政府出台《关于到本世纪末稳定解决全省贫困人口温饱问题的决定》。

全省贫困地区各级党委、政府把扶贫开发作为首要任务，明确党政一把手负全责，开始实行"三定一帮"责任制，"三定"就是定贫困乡、村，定目标任务，定完成任务时间，"一帮"就是帮助贫困户脱贫。1998年，按照省委、省政府要求，各地开始抽调大批党政机关干部驻村扶贫，这成为促进扶贫工作的有效办法。

在此时期，如何集中力量解决黄河低滩区脱贫致富的问题，是河南扶贫工作的重点之一。河南黄河滩区滩面广阔，是黄河主要的行洪区和蓄洪区，自古以来由于河道淤积，河床不断抬高，洪水漫滩时常发生。同时从1972年始，黄河又反复出现断流现象。恶劣的自然条件，再加上经济与社会发展等方面的不利因素，黄河滩区一直是河南省最贫困的地区之一，黄河滩区的扶贫工作是全国扶贫工作中最难啃的硬骨头之一。

为了改变滩区面貌，从1988年起，河南在中央有关政策和资金的支持下，有计划地开展了滩区水利建设，使黄河滩区的自然条件发生了根本变化。当地农民利用黄河滩区的自然条件，发展特色高效农业、水稻业、养殖业等，促进了农民的增产增收。与省会郑州一河之隔的原阳县，

III. Poverty Alleviation (1994-2000)

In 1994, the State Council launched *The National Seven-year Plan for Poverty Alleviation (1994-2000)*, which committed to gather enough human, material, and financial resources to ensure that the basic needs of 80 million impoverished rural residents would be met in 7 years by the year 2000. At that time, 28 counties in Henan were listed as the key targets of the national support and 6 counties the provincial support.

To implement the strategic decision of the CPC Central Committee and the State Council, Henan provincial Party committee and the government formulated the poverty alleviation plan. In April 1994, the provincial Party committee and the government held a conference on poverty alleviation, development, and rural work, which resolved to ensure the 7.6 million poor population in Henan would have enough food and clothing by the end of the 20th century. In May 1994, the provincial government formulated *The Poverty Alleviation Plan of Henan Province (1994-2000)*. In June 1994, the provincial Party committee and the government issued the *Decisions on the Stable Solution to Ensure the Poor Population in Henan Province Have Enough Food and Clothing by the End of the 20th Century*.

The Party committees and governments at all levels in the poor areas of Henan Province took on poverty alleviation and development as priorities, made it clear that the chief leaders were fully responsible, and began to implement the responsibility system of "three identifying and one assisting." "Three identifying" was to identify the poor towns and villages, set targets, and set the completion time. "One assisting" was to assist the poor households out of poverty. In accordance with the requirements of the provincial Party committee and the government, in 1998 a large number of officials were dispatched to help the poor in villages, which proved to be an effective measure to accelerate poverty alleviation.

In this period, lifting the low beach area of the Yellow River out of poverty was one of the focuses of poverty alleviation in Henan Province. The beach area of the Yellow River in Henan is vast, which is the main flood area and flood

在改革开放之后，较早地发展成为特色农业县，摆脱了贫困。当地的"原阳大米"闻名遐迩，水稻种植业在这段时期成为原阳县农业的支柱产业。同时，原阳是中原地区最大的鸵鸟、乌骨鸡、珍珠鸡等禽类养殖繁育基地，这里的特种水产养殖也发展良好。到1996年，原阳县农民人均纯收入中，来自畜牧业的收入就占了31%。

20世纪90年代，乡镇企业蓬勃发展，开展多种经营，带动了市场繁荣，成为河南人民脱贫致富的有效途径。长垣县通过大力发展乡镇企业，形成防腐、建筑、起重三大支柱产业，业务冲出河南，走向全国。该县的恼里镇，在1980年的时候，粮食平均亩产只有50千克，人均纯收入仅有36元。经过10多年发展，到1997年时，其乡镇企业总数达到1352个，产值突破6亿元，并形成两大企业集团。该镇的小辛庄也成为河南黄河滩区的第一个亿元村，人均收入超过了2900元。

在这个时期，河南扶贫工作成就显著。截至2000年底，全省农村贫困人口由1993年的760万人减少到232万人，贫困人口占全省乡村总人口的比例由1993年的10%下降到1.7%。

storage area. Since ancient times, siltation has caused the riverbed to be rising continuously and flooding often occurs. From 1972, the Yellow River has dried up repeatedly. These harsh natural conditions and adverse factors for economic and social development have made the beach area of the Yellow River one of the poorest places in Henan Province. Poverty alleviation in this area is one of the most difficult to accomplish.

To make a change, Henan Province has carried out water conservancy construction systematically since 1988 with the support of policies and funds given by the central government, fundamentally changing the natural conditions of the Yellow River beach area. Local peasants have made use of the local conditions to develop agriculture, rice planting, husbandry, etc. with characteristics and high efficiency, which increases peasants' yield and income. Yuanyang County, separated from Zhengzhou (capital of Henan Province) by the Yellow River, developed itself into a characteristic agricultural county shortly after the reform and opening-up, and eliminated poverty. "Yuanyang rice" was well-known, and rice planting was the pillar of agriculture in the county during this period. In addition, Yuanyang was the largest breeding base for ostrich, silky fowl, guinea fowl and other poultry in the Central Plains area of China. The special aquaculture there was also developing well. By 1996, the income from husbandry had accounted for 31% of local peasants' per capita net income.

In the 1990s, township enterprises flourished and diversified businesses, which effectively activated the market and enabled Henan's people to overcome poverty and grow rich. Through vigorous development of township enterprises, Changyuan County formed three pillar industries of anti-corrosion, construction and lifting, and their business was expanded to the whole country. In 1980, the average grain yield of Naoli Town, Changyuan County, was only 50 kilograms per *mu* (0.067 hectare), and the per capita net income was only 36 *yuan*. After more than 10 years of development, the total number of township enterprises reached 1,352 in 1997 and the output value exceeded 600 million *yuan*; two corporations came into being. XiaoxinVillage became the first 100-million-*yuan* village in the Yellow River beach area in Henan with a per capita income of more than 2,900 *yuan*.

During this period, poverty alleviation in Henan Province made remarkable

第一章　扶贫道路

电力扶贫——卢氏县（摄影：聂金锋）
Electric power advancement for poverty alleviation—Lushi County (Photographer: Nie Jinfeng)

progress. By the end of 2000, the rural poor population of the province had decreased from 7.6 million in 1993 to 2.32 million, and the proportion of the poor people in the total rural population of the province had dropped from 10% to 1.7%.

四、扶贫开发纲要实施阶段（2001—2012 年）

2001 年，国务院出台《中国农村扶贫开发纲要（2001—2010 年）》，统一了新阶段扶贫开发工作对象的标准。根据这一标准，到 2000 年底，河南省尚未解决温饱问题的贫困人口 232 万、"低收入人口" 598 万，合计 830 万人，占全省乡村人口总数的 10.6%。

2002 年，河南省政府出台《河南省农村扶贫开发规划（2003—2010 年）》，明确 31 个县为河南省新时期国家级扶贫开发工作重点县，同时将山区、黄淮滩区、低洼易涝区等群众生产生活条件恶劣的区域和贫困人口相对集中的 44 个扶贫开发工作重点县、565 个重点乡、10430 个重点村作为扶贫开发的重点范围，继续大力推进扶贫开发。

同"八七扶贫计划"阶段相比，这一时期最大的变化是贫困人口不再像过去集中在贫困县，而是集中在部分贫困村。针对这一变化，中央首先调整了扶贫对象的标准范围，从瞄准贫困县转向瞄准贫困村，开始采用整村推进、分批扶持的办法，对重点贫困村进行集中扶持，以"扶持一村、脱贫一村、巩固一村、致富一村"为目标，有力推动了社会主义新农村建设。其中，洛宁县、民权县被确定为国家连片开发试点县。像洛宁县，2007 年利用中央、市、县财政资金 1400 万元，整合各类涉农资金近 5000 万元，自筹资金 1000 多万元，对 16 个集中连片的贫困村进行扶贫开发和综合治理，使这片原本基础设施落后、脏乱差问题突出、群众致富门路狭窄的区域发生了翻天覆地的变化。水泥路通村入户、联通成网，公共服务设施初步完善，村容村貌整洁美观，村庄周围绿树环绕，主导产业初具规模，群众生活明显改善。16 个村人均年纯收入 3012 元，超过了全县 2746 元的农民人均收入水平，16 个贫困村实现了整体脱贫，效果十分明显。

2003 年开始，国家组织开展以贫困劳动力培训转移为主要内容的"雨

IV. Implementation of the Outline of Development-driven Poverty Alleviation (2001-2012)

In 2001, the State Council issued *The Outline of Rural Poverty Alleviation Development in China (2001-2010)*, setting standards for the targets of poverty alleviation and development for the new stage. According to this standard, 2.32 million poor people still had difficulty with food and clothing and there were 5.98 million low-income people in Henan Province by the end of 2000, making 8.3 million in total and accounting for 10.6% of the rural population in the province.

In 2002, Henan provincial government issued *The Rural Poverty Alleviation and Development Plan of Henan Province (2003-2010)*, listing 31 counties as the key targets of national poverty alleviation and development in Henan Province in the new era. Meanwhile, the government set 44 counties, 565 towns and 10,430 villages located in the mountainous areas, the beach areas between the Yellow River and the Huaihe River, and the low-lying and waterlogging-prone areas where the living conditions were still very harsh and local people lived a poor life as the focus of rural poverty alleviation and development.

Compared with the stage of implementing *The National Seven-year Plan for Poverty Alleviation (1994-2000)*, the biggest change was that the poor people were no longer concentrated in poor counties, but in some poor villages. In response to this, the central government first adjusted the targets of poverty alleviation, from targeting poor counties to poor villages, and began to accelerate poverty alleviation in villages in turn. With the goal of "supporting one village, getting rid of poverty, consolidating achievements and making the village rich," the central government carried out intensive poverty alleviation work in key poverty-stricken villages, which vigorously promoted the construction of new socialist countryside. Luoning County and Minquan County were designated as national pilot counties for contiguous development. In 2007, Luoning County made use of 14 million *yuan* of central, municipal and county fiscal funds, integrated nearly 50 million *yuan* of various agriculture-related funds, and raised more than 10 million *yuan* to carry out poverty alleviation, development, and comprehensive management in 16

露计划"。河南是全国人口大省,同时也是贫困人口和剩余劳动力最多的省份之一。为变人口压力为人力资源优势,河南大胆创新培训机制,突出专业技能培训,加大资金投入,把贫困地区劳动力转移培训作为新阶段扶贫开发的重要工作。仅从 2003 年到 2007 年,河南就累计投入扶贫培训资金 1.98 亿元,建立转移培训基地 216 个,涉及 40 多个专业,年培训能力 30 余万人,培训转移贫困农民 80 万人,劳务输出创收 200 亿元,辐射带动了 1400 万农民增收。

针对自然资源匮乏、生态环境恶劣、生存空间狭小的独居、散居贫困户,河南从 2000 年开始在部分县(市)陆续开展了移民搬迁扶贫开发试点工作,在群众自愿的基础上实行有计划、有组织的搬迁扶贫。2008 年 10 月,国务院扶贫办在洛阳市召开全国移民扶贫工作经验交流会,推广河南省搬迁扶贫的经验和做法。

河南通过"大学生村官计划",实现了全省扶贫开发重点村每个村都有一名大学生的目标,这也为扶贫工作的顺利开展提供了人才保障。

经过扶贫开发纲要在河南十多年的实施推进,全省扶贫工作取得新成效。按照 2000 年国家确定的农民人均年纯收入 865 元的扶贫标准,全省农村贫困人口由 2000 年的 830 万人下降到 2010 年的 224 万人。

contiguous poor villages. This brought about earth-shaking changes in this area where the infrastructure was backward, the surroundings were dirty and messy, and people had few chances to become rich in the past. Now pitch roads connect to each other and link the villages with the outside. Public service facilities are preliminarily improved. The villages are neat and beautiful, surrounded by green trees. The leading industry has begun to take shape, and local people's life has been significantly improved. The per capita annual net income of the 16 villages reaches 3,012 *yuan*, higher than the average annual income of peasants in Luoning County, which is 2,746 *yuan*. The 16 poor villages have shaken off poverty, and the effect of poverty alleviation is impossible to ignore.

From 2003, China has carried out the "rain and dew plan" to help the poverty-stricken laborers through training. Henan Province has a large population, and it is one of the provinces with the largest number of poor people and surplus labor force. To change the population pressure into the advantage of human resources, Henan boldly innovates the training mechanism, highlights training on professional skills, increases the investment on training, and puts the labor transfer and training in poor areas as an important work in the new stage of poverty alleviation and development. From 2003 to 2007, Henan invested 198 million *yuan* in poverty alleviation training, established 216 training centers that could offer more than 40 specialties with an annual training capacity of more than 300,000 people, trained 800,000 poverty-stricken peasants, generated 20 billion *yuan* in labor export, and increased the income of 14 million peasants.

To assist the poor households that were living alone and scattered in poor areas with scarce natural resources, bad ecological environment and narrow living space, Henan Province has carried out the pilot work on migration and poverty alleviation in some counties (cities) since 2000. Driven by the people's own will, well-planned and well-organized relocation and poverty alleviation were implemented. In October 2008, the Poverty Alleviation Office of the State Council held a national conference on relocation and poverty alleviation in Luoyang City, during which the experience and practice of Henan were publicized.

Henan Province has launched "the program of appointing college graduates as village leaders," and achieved its goal of having one college graduate in every

第一章 扶贫道路

易地搬迁扶贫——谷营镇姚寨村建起的新居
Poverty alleviation through relocating poor households—new houses of Yaozhai Village, Guying Town

key village of poverty alleviation and development. This practice guarantees the smooth development of poverty alleviation with ample competent personnel.

After the implementation of *The Outline of Rural Poverty Alleviation and Development in China (2001-2010)* in Henan for more than ten years, new progress was made. According to the poverty alleviation standard determined by the state in 2000—865 *yuan* per capita annual net income, the rural poor population in Henan dropped from 8.3 million in 2000 to 2.24 million in 2010.

五、脱贫攻坚阶段（2013—2020年）

中共十八大以来，以习近平同志为核心的党中央把脱贫攻坚摆到治国理政突出位置，打响了一场脱贫攻坚战，迎来了历史性的跨越和巨变。河南省坚持以习近平新时代中国特色社会主义思想为指导，深入贯彻习近平总书记关于扶贫工作的重要论述和视察河南重要讲话精神，坚决落实党中央、国务院关于打赢脱贫攻坚战的决策部署，完善实行省负总责、市县抓落实、乡村组织实施工作机制，采取超常举措，下足绣花功夫，圆满完成了新时代河南脱贫攻坚各项目标任务，为开启建设现代化河南新征程、谱写中原更加出彩绚丽篇章奠定了坚实基础。

河南成立省委书记、省长任组长的省脱贫攻坚领导小组，组建14个脱贫攻坚重大专项工作指挥部。实行省级领导干部和部分省直单位联系贫困县工作制度，明确37名省级领导干部联系38个国定贫困县、15个省直主要部门联系15个省定贫困县的脱贫攻坚工作。市、县、乡分别建立了领导干部联系帮扶贫困县、乡、村、户制度，落实各项扶贫政策，形成各级党政一把手亲自抓、班子成员按照分工具体抓、省市县乡村五级书记一起抓的攻坚责任制，为打好脱贫攻坚战提供了坚强的政治保证和组织保证。

河南脱贫攻坚的投入力度不断加大。据统计，仅2016年到2020年，共投入财政专项扶贫资金727亿元，53个贫困县和10个参照县统筹整合财政涉农资金1073亿元。全省累计发放扶贫小额贷款615.32亿元，惠及146.43万贫困户。宅基地复垦券累计成交金额300多亿元，全部用于脱贫攻坚。

V. The Battle against Poverty (2013-2020)

Since the 18th CPC National Congress of 2012, the Party Central Committee under the leadership of Xi Jinping has put poverty alleviation as the focus of governance, launched a battle against poverty, and brought about a historic leap and great changes. Henan Province closely adheres to Xi Jinping's thought on socialism with Chinese characteristics for a new era, implements thoroughly the important statements of General Secretary Xi Jinping on poverty alleviation and his important speech on inspection of Henan Province, carries out resolutely the decisions of the Central Committee and the State Council on winning the battle against poverty, and practices the three-level mechanism. After taking outstanding measures and making meticulous efforts, Henan Province has successfully completed various targets of poverty alleviation and laid a solid foundation for starting a new journey of building modern and prosperous Henan.

Henan set up a provincial leading group for poverty alleviation with the secretary of the provincial Party committee and the governor as the leaders, and established 14 headquarters for key poverty alleviation tasks. The provincial officials and some government-affiliated institutions should be responsible for the poverty-stricken counties. In this way, 37 provincial officials were responsible for 38 state-determined poor counties, and 15 main provincial government-affiliated institutions were responsible for 15 province-determined poor counties respectively. Soon the system of responsibility was established, that is, leaders of cities, counties and towns assisted certain poverty-stricken counties, villages and families respectively, and various poverty alleviation policies were implemented. Leaders of the Party and the government took overall responsibility, team members were responsible for the specific work, and the secretaries of the province, cities, counties and villages were jointly responsible, providing a strong political and organizational guarantee for the fight against poverty.

Henan Province kept putting more funds into poverty alleviation year by year. According to statistics, from 2016 to 2020 a total of 72.7 billion *yuan* of special poverty alleviation funds were invested, and 107.3 billion *yuan* of

河南省脱贫攻坚第一次推进会议
The first conference on poverty alleviation in Henan Province

河南选拔出大量精锐干部直接充实到贫困村。到 2020 年，累计选派驻村干部 13.76 万人，其中第一书记 3.85 万人次，实现对建档立卡贫困村、党组织软弱涣散村、艾滋病防治帮扶重点村全覆盖。严格落实"队员当代表、单位做后盾、领导负总责"工作机制和"五天四夜"驻村制，开展年度绩效考核，确保真帮实扶。在所有贫困村和脱贫任务较重的非贫困村建立 4.2 万个村级脱贫责任组，一大批优秀党员干部投身脱贫攻坚一线。坚持把大别山区、伏牛山区、太行山区和黄河滩区作为脱贫攻坚主战场，瞄准突出问题和薄弱环节集中发力。

agriculture-related funds were integrated in 53 poor counties and 10 relative poor counties. Henan issued 61.532 billion *yuan* of small loans for poverty alleviation, benefiting 1.4643 million poverty-stricken households. The total transaction of homestead reclamation bonds reached more than 30 billion *yuan*, all of which were used to fight poverty.

Henan selected a large number of competent officials to work in the poor villages. By 2020, a total of 137,600 village officials had been selected and dispatched, including 38,500 first secretaries of village Party committees. Registered poor villages, villages with weak Party organizations, and key villages of AIDS prevention and assistance were fully covered. In practice, the working mechanism—"team members are representatives, units are backings, and leaders take overall responsibility" and officials stay at villages "five days and four nights" every week—was strictly implemented. And annual performance appraisal was carried out to ensure the effectiveness of assistance. Henan established 42,000 village-level poverty relief responsibility groups in all poor villages and non-poor villages with heavy poverty relief tasks, and a large number of outstanding CPC members and officials engaged in the front line of poverty alleviation. The Dabie Mountain, the Funiu Mountain, the Taihang Mountain and the Yellow River beach areas have long been primary battlefields for poverty alleviation, and additional efforts have been made to solve the prominent problems and weaknesses there.

Over the years, great changes have taken place in the poverty-stricken areas and in people's life by means of continuous infrastructure improvement and solid development or relocation of industry. Since 2016, a total of 319 kilometers of expressways have been constructed, 40,500 kilometers of newly-reconstructed rural roads and 1,908 kilometers of ordinary trunk roads have been built in the poor counties of Henan Province. All villages have pitch roads and villagers can travel outside their village by bus. Roads have been built into the deep mountains and pass through the doors of farmhouses, paving the way for the villagers to shake off poverty and build a better life.

Through strengthening the organization of the Party and promoting poverty alleviation, the cohesion and capability of rural grassroots Party organizations have been improved. A total of 11,300 weak and loose village Party organizations

《人民日报》报道兰考脱贫
The reports of Lankao's poverty alleviation on *People's Daily*

通过不断完善贫困地区基础设施，扎实开展产业扶贫、易地搬迁扶贫等工作，使贫困地区的面貌和贫困群众的生产生活发生了翻天覆地的变化。2016年以来，河南贫困县累计新增高速公路319千米，新改建农村公路4.05万千米、普通干线公路1908千米，全省行政村通硬化路率、具备条件的行政村通客车率均达到100%，一条条致富路通到大山深处、修到了家门口，为乡亲们铺就了脱贫致富奔小康的康庄大道。

通过抓党建促脱贫攻坚，提高了农村基层党组织的凝聚力、战斗力，累计排查整顿1.13万个软弱涣散村党组织，提升了基层治理能力和管理水平。持续开展"听党话、感党恩、跟党走"活动和脱贫政策、脱贫故事、脱贫经验宣讲活动，推广"爱心超市""孝善基金"等做法，探索"红黑榜"扶志模式，教育引导贫困群众自强不息、勤劳致富。累计

have been investigated and rectified, so that the grassroots governance and management level have been raised. We continue carrying out the activities of "listening to the Party's words, appreciating the Party's kindness and following the Party" and publicize our poverty alleviation policies, stories and experience. We also promote the "benevolence supermarket" and "filial piety fund," use the "red and black list" to inspire people, and educate and guide the poverty-stricken people to strive for self-improvement and prosperity. A total of 51,100 villagers in the poor villages have been cultivated to play a leading role in the fight against poverty. For the poor people able to work, we provide training on practical skills, market operation, and employment and entrepreneurship that can enhance their self-development. With the help of the Party, the government and all walks of life, the poor people have changed their ideas, enhanced their ability for development, and boosted their motivation to get rid of poverty. They pursue a happy life through their own efforts.

Henan Province has made solid efforts to build a "Trinity" pattern of special poverty alleviation, industrial support for poverty alleviation and social poverty alleviation. All sectors of the society widely participate in and support poverty alleviation. Various actions are carried out steadily. For example, "thousands of enterprises assisting thousands of villages," "the 'ten thousand' project of assigning science and technology commissioners to support poverty alleviation in Henan," "the smart daughters-in-law" project organized by the Women's Federation, labor models of the trade union pitching in poverty alleviation, "help coming from all quarters" organized by Henan Communist Youth League, "ten million" project of poverty alleviation through which provincial government-affiliated institutions and poor villages, Party branches and poor households, Party members and students from the poor families become pairs respectively, and "consumption for poverty alleviation," through which social forces participate in the fight against poverty.

Under the leadership of the Party Central Committee and the State Council and through the unremitting efforts of Henan Province, a decisive victory in poverty alleviation has been achieved. A total of 7.186 million registered poor people have been lifted out of poverty, 9,536 poor villages have eliminated poverty, all of the 53 poor counties have been lifted out of poverty, regional poverty problems have been effectively solved, and absolute poverty has been abolished in Henan.

培育贫困村致富带头人 5.11 万名，带动贫困群众脱贫增收。对有劳动能力的贫困群众，加强实用技能、市场经营、就业创业等培训，提高自我发展能力。贫困群众在党和政府、社会各界大力帮扶下，思想观念进一步转变，发展能力进一步增强，脱贫干劲进一步提升，不等不靠，主动作为，用勤劳双手去创造幸福美好生活。

河南省扎实推进构建专项扶贫、行业扶贫、社会扶贫"三位一体"大扶贫格局。社会各界广泛参与、支持脱贫攻坚，"千企帮千村"精准扶贫行动扎实推进，"河南省科技特派员助力脱贫攻坚'十百千'工程"深入实施，妇联系统"巧媳妇"工程不断拓展，工会系统劳模助力脱贫攻坚行动全面展开，"八方援"河南共青团助力脱贫攻坚行动深入开展，"省直机关百千万工程助力脱贫计划"有效实施，省直单位与贫困村、机关党支部与贫困户、机关党员与贫困家庭学生结成帮扶对子常态化开展帮扶，"消费扶贫"也成为社会力量参与脱贫攻坚的重要途径。

在党中央、国务院领导下，经过全省上下不懈努力，河南脱贫攻坚取得了决定性胜利。全省共实现 718.6 万建档立卡贫困人口脱贫，9536 个贫困村全部退出贫困序列，53 个贫困县全部脱贫摘帽，区域性贫困问题有效解决，绝对贫困人口全部清零。

第二章

攻坚历程

Chapter II

The Course of Poverty Alleviation

一、坚持一个方略：精准扶贫

【故事】精准扶贫给李小山带来新生活

李小山的家在焦作市博爱县柏山镇酒奉村，家中有 5 口人。李小山的双胞胎儿子出生时患有脑瘫，生活无法自理，只能由妻子杜素清专门负责照顾。前几年，女儿正在上大学，家庭收入全靠李小山一人打拼，生活的重担压得夫妻俩喘不过气来。

按照"扶持对象"精准的要求，2017 年 5 月，李小山一家被正式评定为建档立卡贫困户。李小山一度觉得很没面子，整天愁眉苦脸，不想见人。

驻酒奉村的博爱县纪委监委脱贫责任组了解到李小山的情况后，精准施策，主动邀请他参加镇里、村上组织的座谈会、培训会，驻村第一书记李卫东也多次到他家中走访，和他促膝谈心，打消他的思想顾虑，并根据他家的实际情况为他办理了低保、残疾人两项补贴，并落实了助学补助、健康扶贫等优惠政策。在大家的不懈努力下，李小山逐步感受到了温暖的关怀，他感慨地说："精准扶贫的好政策就是我的靠山，我再不努力实在说不过去。"

酒奉村脱贫责任组了解到李小山会点修车技术，就专门在村口给他设置了固定摊位。刚开始时李小山生意很少，他就主动和经过的行人打招呼，同街坊邻居唠家常；顾客修完车发现钱不够了，他就让人家先走，下次再给；平时电动车充气、简单的维修，无论认识与否他一概不收钱。李小山的"生意经"看似吃了亏，却积攒了人气，赢得了顾客。渐渐地，他的生意有了起色，每月仅补胎的收入就已经从刚开始的 100 多元增长到近千元。

李小山颇具生意头脑，又能吃苦耐劳，修车空当，他还开三轮车给别人送水、送饮料，有人需要拉货，他就用三轮车帮忙去送。李卫东把

I. Adhering to One Strategy: Targeted Poverty Alleviation

【Case】Targeted Poverty Allevation Helping Li Xiaoshan Live a New Life

Li Xiaoshan lives in Jiufeng Village of Baishan Town, Boai County, Jiaozuo City, with five members of his family. Li Xiaoshan's twin sons were born with cerebral palsy and his wife, Du Suqing, must look after them every day. Several years ago, Xiaoshan and Suqing's daughter was studying in university and the family depended on Li Xiaoshan alone for an income. The burden of life was too heavy for the couple.

According to the targeted poverty alleviation policy, Li Xiaoshan's family was a poverty-stricken household in May 2017. For a time, Li Xiaoshan felt very embarrassed for his poverty, so he worried all day long and refused to see anyone.

After learning about Li Xiaoshan's condition, the poverty alleviation responsibility group in the village, which was made up of Boai County Commission for Discipline Inspection and Supervision, invited Xiaoshan to participate in seminars and trainings organized by the town and village. Li Weidong, first secretary of the village, visited Li Xiaoshan many times, had heart-to-heart talks with him and banished his worries. Li Weidong helped Li Xiaoshan apply for subsistence allowance, disabled allowance, tuition allowance, and healthcare for his family. After experiencing these unremitting efforts, Li Xiaoshan felt warmed and declared in an emotional voice, "The good policy of targeted poverty alleviation backs me up. I must make my own efforts."

The poverty alleviation responsibility group learned that Li Xiaoshan could repair bikes, so they set up a fixed stall for him at the entrance of the village. At first, though Li Xiaoshan had little business, he greeted the passers-by friendly and chatted with neighbors. Whenever customers did not have enough money after their bikes were repaired, he let them go and pay next time. He offered free tire inflation to people. It seemed that Li Xiaoshan was taking losses, but in fact he won the favor of customers. His business became better gradually, and he went from earning little more than 100 *yuan* to nearly 1,000 *yuan* each month just by repairing tires.

李小山的努力都看在眼里，通过积极争取，又帮他申请了代销古温酒的扶贫岗。

李小山(摄影：程全)
Li Xiaoshan (Photographer: Cheng Quan)

2018 年底，李小山一家人均纯收入 5800 元，成功脱贫。为了稳固扶贫成果，防止返贫，2019 年 8 月，驻村工作队帮李小山申请到了 3 万元政府贴息贷款，用于扩大经营。

不怕苦，不嫌累，不管什么活儿，李小山都乐意干。如今，虽然每天忙忙碌碌，但是李小山过得充实、快乐。

【全景】精准扶贫是打赢脱贫攻坚战的制胜法宝

党的十八大以来，河南省委、省政府贯彻落实习近平总书记关于实施精准扶贫的原则要求，实行扶持对象、项目安排、资金使用、措施到户、因村派人、脱贫成效"六个精准"，实行发展生产、易地搬迁、生

Li Xiaoshan was skilled at business and worked hard. When he had free time, he delivered drinking water, beverages, and goods with a tricycle to earn extra money. Li Weidong saw Li Xiaoshan's efforts and helped him to apply for the poverty alleviation post of selling Guwen (a brand of Jiaozuo) wine.

At the end of 2018, the per capita net income of Li Xiaoshan's family was 5,800 *yuan* and his family was free from poverty. To maintain the success of poverty alleviation and prevent this family from falling into poverty again, in August 2019 the village-based work team in the village helped Li Xiaoshan apply for a discount loan of 30,000 *yuan* offered by the government to expand his business.

Li Xiaoshan is willing to do different kinds of work no matter how hard and tiring. Now he is busy and happy every day.

【Panorama】Targeted Poverty Alleviation: the Magic Weapon to Win the Battle against Poverty

Since the 18th CPC National Congress, Henan provincial Party committee and the provincial government have implemented General Secretary Xi Jinping's principles on targeted poverty alleviation, targeting "six precision" in aspects of poverty alleviation, project arrangement, fund utilization, relief measures to households, dispatch of working team and the effect of poverty alleviation, and carried out "five measures" of developing production, relocation, eco-compensation, developing education and social security. Based on the real conditions of Henan, the provincial Party committee and the government focus on "whom to support, who will support, how to support and how to exit," and transform scattered to targeted poverty relief.

We have made accurate identification of "whom to support." To assure targeted support and policy implementation, the Information Center on Poverty Alleviation and Development of Henan Province was established in 2014 and worked on poverty registration and accurate identification of the poverty-stricken people. In 2015, Henan took the lead in formulating *The Plan for Checking the Registered Poor People in Henan Province* and organized the "follow-up" checks to ensure the accuracy of poverty identification.

We build the grassroots Party organization well for "who will support." In

态补偿、发展教育、社会保障兜底"五个一批",结合全省实际,在解决好"扶持谁、谁来扶、怎么扶、如何退"的问题上下足绣花功夫,实现了从大水漫灌向精准滴灌的转变。

围绕解决"扶持谁"的问题,做好精准识别。为做好精准帮扶、精准施策,2014年成立了河南省扶贫开发信息中心,推动开展建档立卡工作,精准找出贫困对象。2015年,在全国率先制定《河南省扶贫开发建档立卡贫困人口复核工作实施方案》,组织开展贫困人口精准识别"回头看",确保识别精准度。

围绕解决"谁来扶"的问题,建好基层党组织。2015年省委组织部、省委农办、省扶贫办联合出台《关于全面开展选派机关优秀干部到村任第一书记工作的实施意见》,2018年进一步出台《关于进一步加强贫困村驻村工作队选派管理工作的通知》。在全省所有贫困村和扶贫任务较重的非贫困村建立4.2万个村级脱贫责任组,由乡镇副科级以上干部任组长,统筹抓好脱贫攻坚各项工作。

驻村第一书记在扶贫基地与群众交谈

The first secretary of the village is talking to a villager at the poverty alleviation base.

2015, the Organization Department, the Agricultural Affairs Office and the Poverty Alleviation Office of Henan provincial Party committee jointly issued *The Opinions on Selecting and Dispatching Outstanding Officials to Villages as the First Secretary*, and in 2018 issued *The Notice on Strengthening the Management of Selecting and Dispatching the Resident Working Teams to Poor Villages*. 42,000 village-level poverty relief responsibility groups were formed in all poor villages and non-poor villages with heavy poverty alleviation tasks in Henan Province, with officials at or above the township deputy level as the group leaders to take overall responsibilities to tackle the key problems in poverty alleviation.

We implement precies policies for "how to support." In 2016, on the basis of *The Opinions of Henan Provincial Party Committee and Provincial Government on Winning the Battle against Poverty Alleviation*, the offices of Henan provincial Party committee and provincial government issued "five measures" on accurate identification of poverty alleviation targets, "five programs" on poverty alleviation through rural labor migration and "five special programs" on poverty alleviation by developing education; a poverty alleviation system of "1 + 15" came into being. In 2017, the provincial government further refined policy implementing measures and issued 53 supporting policies. In 2018, the provincial government-affiliated institutions refined the industry poverty alleviation policies and improved the standardization and institutionalization of poverty alleviation work according to *The Three-year Plan for Winning the Battle against Poverty in Henan Province*. In 2019, Henan provincial Party committee and provincial government issued *Opinions on Consolidating the Achievements of Poverty Alleviation and Effectively Preventing the Return of Poverty*, and the provincial leading group for poverty alleviation issued *The Plan on "Follow-up" Checks of Poverty Alleviation in Henan Province*. The two documents aimed at making up for weaknesses and improving the quality of poverty alleviation. In 2020, the provincial leading group for poverty alleviation issued *Measures for Supporting Poverty Alleviation in Key Counties and Villages That Are Still in Poverty* and *Opinions on Strengthening Poverty Alleviation Among Registered Poor Households and Marginal Households and Effectively Preventing the Return of Poverty and New Poverty* to gather efforts to conquer the last fortress of the battle against poverty and consolidate forces to achieve complete poverty alleviation.

围绕解决"怎么扶"的问题,做好精准施策。2016年,在出台《中共河南省委 河南省人民政府关于打赢脱贫攻坚战的实施意见》的基础上,省委办公厅、省政府办公厅出台扶贫对象精准识别等"5个办法"、转移就业脱贫等"5个方案"、教育脱贫等"5个专项方案",形成了"1+15"脱贫攻坚政策体系。2017年,省级进一步细化实化政策措施,研究出台53个配套政策文件。2018年,围绕落实《河南省打赢脱贫攻坚战三年行动计划》,省直有关单位细化完善行业扶贫政策,提升扶贫工作规范化、标准化、制度化水平。2019年,省委、省政府出台《关于巩固脱贫成果有效防止返贫的意见》,省脱贫攻坚领导小组出台《河南省脱贫攻坚"回头看"工作方案》,着力补齐短板弱项,提高脱贫质量。2020年,省脱贫攻坚领导小组出台《关于支持脱贫攻坚重点县和未脱贫村脱贫攻坚若干措施》《关于加强脱贫监测户边缘户帮扶有效防止返贫和新致贫的意见》等政策文件,聚力攻克最后堡垒,巩固脱贫成果。

围绕解决"如何退"的问题,严把退出关。明确贫困退出标准和程序,严把退出关口。2016年出台《河南省贫困退出实施办法》,建立严格、规范、透明的贫困退出机制。2018年制定实施《省脱贫攻坚领导小组关于加强对贫困县退出工作指导的意见》。根据国家第三方评估结果显示,全省贫困人口退出准确率由2016年的98.59%提高到2019年的100%。

We should keep strict control and make clear criteria and procedures for "how to exit from poverty." In 2016, *Measures for Exiting from Poverty in Henan Province* was issued, which set a strict, standardized, and open poverty exiting mechanism. In 2018, *Opinions Proposed by the Provincial Leading Group on Poverty Alleviation on Strengthening the Guidance for Exiting from the List of Poor Counties* was formulated and implemented. According to the results released by national third-party evaluation, the accuracy of the poor people lifted from poverty in Henan Province increased from 98.59% in 2016 to 100% in 2019.

二、高举一面旗帜：兰考县

【故事】张庄村："幸福村"里的"成绩单"

张庄村，地处九曲黄河最后一道弯，曾是兰考县最大的风口。20世纪60年代，焦裕禄在此治理风沙，让当地群众结束了逃荒的历史。然而，到21世纪初，张庄村仍然没有摆脱贫困。

2014年，711户2963口人的张庄村，在册贫困户207户754人，是远近闻名的贫困村。

要说张庄村是如何从贫困村变成了"幸福村"，还要从2014年3月17日这一天说起。

那一天，习近平总书记来到了河南兰考县张庄村，走进村民家，与乡亲们聊家常，和干部们谈工作，鼓励大家共同努力，早日脱贫奔小康。

那时候，闫春光是张庄村的贫困户，他养鸡遭遇挫折，欠下几万元的外债。家里上有80多岁的奶奶，下有两个嗷嗷待哺的小孩。

"多亏县里的好政策，拿到了5万元无息贷款，还有人提供技术指导。"闫春光所说的无息贷款，得益于兰考县的金融扶贫政策。

勤快建鸡棚、虚心学技术、逐步上规模……闫春光的蛋鸡养殖场规模从2014年的1000只，发展到2018年的1万只，2018年鸡场纯收入30万元。

闫春光没有止步，不仅把手里的钱投资租厂房、买设备，又从银行贷出8万元，用古法加工芝麻油、花生油、红薯粉条等。

像闫春光一样的张庄人埋头苦干，在县乡村的统一部署下，通过不同的方式走上了脱贫道路。

II. Holding Up a Banner: Lankao County

【Case】 Zhangzhuang Village: "Report Card" of the "Happy Village"

Zhangzhuang Village is located in the last bend of the Yellow River and once suffered sandstorms most severely in Lankao County. In the 1960s, Jiao Yulu worked hard to control sandstorms there and since then local people did not have to fear famine any longer. However, this village was still in poverty at the beginning of the 21st century.

In 2014, Zhangzhuang Village had 711 households and 2,963 people, among whom there were 207 registered poor households and 754 poor people. Zhangzhuang was a well-known poor village.

To see how Zhangzhuang Village has been transformed from a poor village to a "happy village," we have to start on March 17, 2014.

On that day, General Secretary Xi Jinping came to inspect Zhangzhuang Village. He went into villagers' home, chatted with them, and talked with local officials. Xi encouraged everyone to make efforts together to get rid of poverty and live a better life as soon as possible.

Yan Chunguang's family was poor. He failed raising chickens and owed tens of thousands *yuan* in debt. His grandmother was over 80 years old and Yan had two babies at home to be fed.

"Thanks to the good policy of the county, I got an interest-free loan of 50,000 *yuan* and received technical guidance," Yan later said. The interest-free loan mentioned by Yan Chunguang was provided by the financial poverty alleviation program of Lankao County.

Supported by the loan, Yan Chunguang worked hard to build chicken sheds, learned techniques modestly, and gradually expanded his business. The number of laying hens on his farm increased from 1,000 in 2014 to 10,000 in 2018, and Yan ended 2018 with a net income of 300,000 *yuan*.

Yan Chunguang did not stop. He not only invested his money in renting factories and buying equipment, but also borrowed 80,000 *yuan* from the bank to develop new businesses—producing sesame oil, peanut oil, and sweet potato noodles.

张庄村幸福路
Xingfu Road of Zhangzhuang Village

张庄村鼓励村民把自有的闲置院落改为民宿，免费提供设计方案，房租收益全归各家各户，40多户村民陆续办起农家乐，走上了脱贫致富之路；整理土地，建成近200个哈密瓜种植大棚；建设村头扶贫车间，传承当地的红薯醋加工工艺；流转100多亩荒滩地，引进白对虾养殖产业；引入一家"新三板"菌类养殖加工企业入驻张庄村。

2017年3月，张庄村与兰考县一齐摘掉了贫困的帽子。

2018年，张庄村人均纯收入从2014年的4900元增加到11600元，村集体收入从零增长到40余万元。

脱贫当年，张庄村把村里的主干道取名为幸福路，同时引导村民重新设计翻修路两旁的旧宅老院，建成门面房对外出租。2020年的幸福路两旁，红墙黛瓦、装饰古朴的店铺开门迎客，印有花生糕的招牌在阳光下熠熠生辉；三五成群的中年妇女聚集在张庄布鞋的手工坊，一针一线纳起千层底；春光油坊的芝麻油飘出阵阵醇香，弥散整条街道……

The villagers of Zhangzhuang Village worked as hard as Yan Chunguang. Under the unified leadership of the county, town and village, they abolished poverty in many ways.

Zhangzhuang Village encouraged villagers to change their own idle courtyard into holiday hotels and provided free construction designs to them. These rentals belonged to each household. More than 40 households established farm stays, escaped poverty, and gradually became wealthy. Villagers cleared land and built nearly 200 greenhouses for planting Hami melons. They built a poverty alleviation workshop at the entrance of the village to produce vinegar according to their traditional sweet potato processing technique. Villagers transformed more than 100 *mu* (6.7 hectares) of wasteland into white prawn breeding ponds. They also introduced a fungus cultivating and processing enterprise to the village.

In March 2017, Zhangzhuang Village and Lankao County abolished poverty together.

The per capita net income of Zhangzhuang Village increased from 4,900 *yuan* in 2014 to 11,600 *yuan* in 2018, and the collective income of the village increased from zero to more than 400,000 *yuan*.

In 2017, Zhangzhuang Village named its main road Xingfu Road, and led villagers to redesign and renovate the old houses on both sides of the road. Rooms behind the newly-built facade were rented as shops. In 2020, shops with red walls and ancient decorations on both sides of Xingfu Road opened for business. Signs for peanut cakes now gleam in the sunshine, middle-aged women gather in the handcraft shop of cloth shoes, stitching the multi-layer soles, and fragrance of sesame oil wafts out of Chunguang oil shop and perfumes the whole street.

【Case】Zhaoduolou Village: Regaining the Red Flag

On March 4, 2019, three or four thousand people attended a three-level officials' conference in Lankao County. Meanwhile, a video conference was held in 16 towns of Lankao County. At the conference, Wang Song, who would later be the Party secretary of Zhaoduolou Village, Putaojia Town, handed over a red flag with "red-flag village for grassroots Party construction" to leaders gathered on the rostrum.

The red flag returned by Wang Song was not ordinary.

【故事】赵垛楼村：失而复得的红旗

2019年3月4日，兰考县三级干部会议，三四千人现场参会；同时，兰考县16个乡镇各有一个视频分会场。会议现场，即将担任兰考县葡萄架乡赵垛楼村村支书的王松将一面写有"基层党建红旗村"的红旗交到主席台上。

王松交回的红旗可不是一面普通的红旗。

在焦裕禄书记带领群众战"三害"的艰苦奋斗中，产生了著名的"四面红旗"，分别是赵垛楼的干劲、韩村的精神、双杨树的道路、秦寨的决心。赵垛楼是当年的"四面红旗"村之一。

20世纪60年代初，焦裕禄书记住在赵垛楼村。洪水到来时，为了看清洪水的流向，雨下得越大，焦书记越是打着雨伞往外跑；哪里水深，他就拿着棍子在水里探、在水里试，最深的水没过了焦书记的腰。在赵垛楼，焦裕禄画出了用来疏通洪水要挖的50多条河沟的位置。

1963年五六月份，赵垛楼人靠着最简单的工具——铁锹，一个月就把50多条河沟全部挖成，这就是赵垛楼的干劲。当年，赵垛楼就产粮食4万千克。

学习焦裕禄的做法，2016年6月，兰考县设立了新时代的"四面红旗"：基层党建红旗村、脱贫攻坚红旗村、乡风文明红旗村、美丽乡村红旗村。

2016年12月，赵垛楼这个老红旗村又成为新红旗村——基层党建红旗村。

2019年3月，因党建工作不力，赵垛楼丢了红旗。于是，有了王松在全县三级干部大会上交回红旗的一幕。

王松，"90后"青年，是村里的能人，开有一家石料厂、一家粮食收购店，解决了30多位村民就业。2019年4月，王松被推选为赵垛楼村支书。上任后，憋足了劲儿的王松甩开膀子大干起来。

In the arduous struggle against the "three natural disasters" led by Secretary Jiao Yulu, Jiao announced that four kinds of outstanding exertion should be prized—the so-called "four red flags," namely the ambitious and passionate drive of Zhaoduolou Village, the high morale of Hancun Village, the strategic orientation of Shuangyangshu Village, and the irreversible determination of Qinzhai Village. Zhaoduolou Village was one of the "four red-flag villages."

In the early 1960s, Secretary Jiao Yulu lved in Zhaoduolou Village. During the flood period, Secretary Jiao ran outside with an umbrella to make clear the direction of the flood, no matter how heavy the rain was. He carried a stick to measure the flood depth and the deepest water covered his waist. In Zhaoduolou Village, Jiao Yulu mapped the location of more than 50 ditches to dredge the flood.

In May and June 1963, the villagers of Zhaoduolou dug up more than 50 ditches in a month with the simplest tool—shovels, showing the passionate drive of the village. In the same year, the whole village produced 40,000 kilograms of grain.

In June 2016, Lankao County set the "four red flags" in the new era: red flag village for grassroots Party construction, red flag village for poverty alleviation, red flag village for rural civilization, and red flag village for beautiful countryside.

In December 2016, Zhaoduolou, the old red flag village, became the new red flag village—the red flag village for grassroots Party construction.

王松学习脱贫攻坚政策，请老党员讲焦裕禄书记的故事；村干部围绕强村富民的共识，明思路、紧人心、促发展、组建党员志愿服务队等。

赵垛楼村领导班子思想统一后，各项工作很快打开局面。

2019年，蜜瓜大棚从110多座增加到153座；发展了300亩精品红薯，售价是普通红薯的3倍多；带动村民养起了构树鸡，3斤以上的鸡每只能卖到50多元，是普通鸡售价的两倍多；村民养羊从1000多只发展到5000多只……

为促进产业发展，赵垛楼一名党员帮扶一名贫困户。慢慢地，赵垛楼返乡创业的人越来越多，村民们对家乡的自豪感越来越强。

2019年7月，赵垛楼村又把失去的红旗领了回来。

【故事】徐场村：琴瑟雅音奏响"富民曲"

琴是中国古代文化地位较高的乐器，位列四艺"琴棋书画"之首。一把古琴，一盏清茶，一只冉冉生烟的檀香，仿佛世界都能得到沉静。

在兰考县堌阳镇徐场村，徐冰和徐亚冲两兄弟经营着一家墨武古琴坊。徐亚冲与古琴的渊源起于2008年北京奥运会。开幕式当天他第一次在电视上听到了古琴的声音，嘈嘈切切错杂弹，仿佛是大珠小珠落玉盘。自此，他便与古琴结下了不解之缘。

为了学习制作古琴，徐亚冲辗转扬州、开封、北京、上海、广州和武当山等地拜师学艺。古人的制琴方法深深影响了他。除了用鹿角打磨琴身，古法制琴还有很多千年流传下来的工序：将绿松石碾碎后涂抹在琴身上，用粉末填充泡桐中细微的孔，用麻布包裹泡桐制作的古琴，用古琴谱印制古琴盖布……

在徐场村，徐亚冲兄弟的古琴制作主要原材料，来自焦裕禄带领兰考人栽下的泡桐树。

20世纪60年代，为了防治风沙，焦裕禄带领兰考人种下500余万株泡桐树。泡桐树耐沙荒、耐盐碱、耐干旱，改善了兰考的生态环境。

红旗失而复得
Regain the red flag

In March 2019, Zhaoduolou Village lost its red flag after poor work in Party construction, hence the above scene of Wang Song returning the red flag at the conference in the present of the whole county.

Wang Song, who was born in the 1990s, is a capable villager. He has a stone material factory and a grain purchasing shop, which provide employment for more than 30 villagers. In April 2019, Wang Song was elected as Party secretary of Zhaoduolou Village. After taking office, he rolled up sleeves and worked hard.

Wang Song studied the policies of poverty alleviation and asked the veteran Party members to recall the story of Secretary Jiao Yulu. Village leaders focused on how to strengthen the village and enrich the people. They cleared thought, gathered people, promoted development, and organized Party members to set up a volunteer service team.

After the leaders of Zhaoduolou Village unified thoughts, all kinds of work were carried out smoothly.

In 2019, the number of melon greenhouses increased from more than 110 to

第二章 攻坚历程

　　80年代，一位上海乐器师傅发现，长在黄河故道沙土中的泡桐，透气性好、共鸣性强、纹理美观，适合做民族乐器。这位乐器师傅在徐场村找到了从事桐木板材加工的代士永，此后，代士永成为上海乐器厂的原材料供应商。与乐器厂深入接触后，代士永决心独立办厂。1988年，他在兰考开办了第一家制造乐器的中州民族乐器厂。

制作民族乐器
Making national musical instruments

153; 300 *mu* (20.1 hectares) of lands were planted with fine sweet potatoes whose price is more than three times that of ordinary ones; villagers were encouraged to raise Broussonetia papyrifera chickens, and each chicken (over 1.5 kg) can be sold for more than 50 *yuan*, twice that of ordinary chicken; the number of sheep fed by villagers increased from 1,000 to more than 5,000.

To promote industrial development, one Party member in the village helped one poor family. Then a cascade of villagers returned home to start their own business and they became proud of their hometown day by day.

In July 2019, Zhaoduolou Village regained the red flag.

【Case】 Xuchang Village: "Song of Prosperity" out of the Elegant Qin

Qin is a musical instrument with high cultural status in ancient China, ranking first among the four arts "qin, chess, calligraphy and painting." With a guqin, a cup of tea and buring sandalwood in the room, the world seems to be tranquil.

Xu Bing and Xu Yachong are brothers, running Mowu Guqin Workshop in Xuchang Village, Guyang Town, Lankao County. Xu Yachong got to know guqin from the 2008 Beijing Olympic Games. On the day of the opening ceremony, he heard guqin on TV for the first time. It sounded to him like big and small pearls falling on a jade plate. Since then, he has been fascinated by guqin.

Xu Yachong went to Yangzhou, Kaifeng, Beijing, Shanghai, Guangzhou and the Wudang Mountain to learn how to make guqin. He was deeply influenced by the ancient method of making qin. In addition to polishing qin with antlers, there are many other procedures that have been handed down for thousands of years: grinding turquoise and smearing it on the qin, filling the tiny holes in Paulownia with powder, wrapping the guqin made of Paulownia with hemp cloth, and printing cover cloth with guqin score…

The main raw materials for making guqin are Paulownias planted by Lankao people under the leadership of Jiao Yulu.

In the 1960s, to control sandstorms, Jiao Yulu led Lankao people to plant more than 5 million Paulownia saplings which were resistant to sand, salt, and drought. Since then, the ecological environment of Lankao has been improved.

In the 1980s, a musical instrument master from Shanghai discovered that

最开始，徐场村的乐器销售主要依靠口碑相传，但传播范围有限，且交通不便、资金匮乏，乐器生产停留在小作坊阶段。2014 年之前，徐场村还是国家级贫困村，生产民族乐器的只有 7 户人家。

为了脱贫攻坚，徐场村决定发挥拥有千亩泡桐木的优势，通过金融贷款支持、申报省级特色旅游村、开发电商等措施，统一技术培训、统一品牌、统一进行农户院墙改造，发展用泡桐木做音板的民族乐器加工业。

在乐器销售上，徐场村也在不断寻找出路，从口碑相传到展会销售，再到线上突围。如今，徐场村的制琴企业搭载电商"这趟快车"把市场拓展至全球各地。

2020 年，徐场村民族乐器生产从业人员超过 1000 人，民族乐器年销售量达 90 万台左右，音板以及配件的年销售量约 100 万套，年均收入约 10 亿元，其中线上销售占比一半。徐场村成为名副其实的"中国民族乐器村"，国内 95% 以上的民族乐器，采用了来自兰考泡桐的音板。

走过风雨，走过春夏秋冬，焦裕禄的功绩依旧造福着兰考人民。一片片泡桐林既防风固沙，也为徐场村摘掉了"贫困帽"，为兰考人民带来了财富。

【全景】"精神高地"走出"经济洼地"

20 世纪 60 年代之前，兰考县有过特别贫穷的岁月，"冬春风沙狂，夏秋水汪汪，一年辛苦半年糠，扶老携幼去逃荒"，就是当时的真实写照。

1964 年，带领兰考群众治理风沙的焦裕禄去世，留下了"亲民爱民、艰苦奋斗、科学求实、迎难而上、无私奉献"的焦裕禄精神。

2002 年，兰考成为国家扶贫开发工作重点县。

2014 年，兰考全面启动脱贫攻坚时，全县还有贫困人口 77350 人，贫困发生率为 10.2%。2014 年 3 月至 5 月，习近平总书记两次考察兰考，兰考做出了"三年脱贫，七年小康"的承诺。

Paulownia growing in the sand of the old course of the Yellow River had good air permeability, strong resonance, and beautiful texture. He realized Paulownia was particularly suitable for making national musical instruments. This master found Dai Shiyong who was engaged in Paulownia processing in Xuchang Village. From then on, Dai Shiyong has become the raw material supplier of Shanghai musical instrument factories. Later, Dai Shiyong decided to run his own factory. In 1988, he opened Zhongzhou National Musical Instrument Factory in Lankao.

At first the sales of musical instruments in Xuchang Village mainly relied on word-of-mouth, but due to the narrow distribution channel, inconvenient transportation and lack of funds, the production of musical instruments was in the stage of small workshops. Before 2014, Xuchang Village was still a state-level poor village with only seven families producing musical instruments.

To abolish poverty, Xuchang Village decided to give full play to the thousand *mu* of Paulownias and develop a national musical instruments processing industry through financial loans, declaration of provincial characteristic tourist village, developing E-commerce, unifying technical training and brand, and rebuilding the walls of villagers' courtyards.

Xuchang Village continued looking for sales channels for its musical instruments, from word-of-mouth to displaying on exhibition, and then online selling. Today, the successful musical instruments factories of Xuchang Village sell their products to the world on the "express train" of E-commerce.

In 2020, there were more than 1,000 people engaged in the production of national musical instruments in Xuchang Village, with an annual sales volume of about 900,000 sets. The annual sales volume of sound boards and accessories were about 1 million sets and the average annual income reached 1 billion *yuan*, of which online sales accounted for half of the total. Xuchang Village has become an authentic "village of national musical instruments." More than 95% of the national musical instruments in China are made of the sound boards processed from Paulownias of Lankao.

Having gone through wind and rain year after year, Jiao Yulu's achievements still benefit the people of Lankao. Paulownia forests not only prevent wind and sand, but also help Xuchang Village eliminate poverty and bring wealth to the people.

兰考脱贫后全民歌唱祖国
Lankao people are singing odes to the motherland after being lifted out of poverty

随后，兰考县探索建立了脱贫攻坚的"12345"工作模式，坚持以脱贫攻坚统揽经济社会发展全局，聚焦产业和就业两个重点不放松，确保了"不落一户、不掉一人"全面脱贫的目标。

兰考县脱贫的具体做法有：全面开展"龙头企业做两端，农民群众干中间，普惠金融惠全链"的带贫增收模式，针对建档立卡贫困户，以发展花生、红薯、苗木、青贮玉米、养羊5种订单农业型产业，瓜菜、养驴、乐器、经济林、食用菌5种能人带动型产业，确保每户至少拥有两项以上增收产业促稳定脱贫。

以"外出务工、产业体系就业、乡镇产业园就近就业、居家灵活就业、公益性岗位就业"五种就业模式，覆盖所有有就业能力、就业意愿、就业条件的贫困家庭。

2017年3月，兰考成为全国首批摘帽的两个国定贫困县之一。

至2020年，兰考县GDP已增加至380亿元，农民人均可支配收入达13126元。

【Panorama】 "Spiritual Highland" out of "Economic Low Land"

Before the 1960s, Lankao County was very poor. The saying that "windy and sandy in winter and spring, watery in summer and autumn; toiling all through the year but only having bran to eat; taking the old and the young to escape from famine" was a true description of that period.

In 1964, Jiao Yulu, the man who led Lankao people to control sandstorm in his lifetime died, but his spirit lived on through his "deep love for people, arduous efforts, scientific integrity, dauntless courage and selfless dedication."

In 2002, Lankao became the key target county of national poverty alleviation and development.

In 2014, when Lankao launched a poverty alleviation campaign, there were 77,350 poor people in the county, and the incidence of poverty was 10.2%. Between March and May in 2014, General Secretary Xi Jinping visited Lankao twice and Lankao made a commitment to "getting rid of poverty in three years and getting into a better-off society in seven."

Soon, Lankao County explored and established the "12345" work mode of poverty alleviation. Lankao insisted on taking poverty alleviation as the key task in the overall development of economy and society, and focused on industry and employment, so as to ensure that the target of poverty alleviation would be achieved in an all-round way, "no household and no one lags behind."

The specific measures of poverty alleviation in Lankao County are as follows: carrying out the mode—"leading enterprises are responsible for investment and distribution channels, peasants work under guidance, and inclusive financial services run through." developing five order-oriented agricultural programs—planting peanuts, sweet potatoes, saplings, silage corns and raising sheep, and five programs derived by capable persons—planting melons and vegetables, raising donkey, making musical instruments, planting economic forests and cultivating edible fungi, so as to ensure that each registered poor household participates in at least two programs to increase income.

Through five modes of employment—"going out to work, employment in the industrial system, employment near the township industrial park, flexible employment at home and employment in public welfare posts," all poor employable and willing families have found work.

演奏自家制作的乐器
Playing the musical instruments made in Xuchang Village

In March 2017, Lankao became the first of the two poverty-stricken counties lifted out of poverty in China.

In 2020, the GDP of Lankao County increased to 38 billion *yuan* and the per capita disposable income of peasants reached 13,126 *yuan*.

三、实施十五个专项行动

1. 产业扶贫

【故事】李德胜和他的百亩"多彩田园"

李德胜是信阳市光山县马畈镇潘楼村李洼村民组的村民。

由于历史原因,李德胜一直没有成家。这个 20 多岁就担任村民组长的汉子,一心扑在侍弄田地上。

2000 年以后,李德胜成了家族留守儿童的大家长:为兄弟、侄子照看孩子。因为没有了主要的收入来源,脱贫攻坚开始后,李德胜被识别为贫困户。

被李德胜照顾的孩子们逐渐长大,去了外地上学,李德胜也被"解放"出来。闲下来的李德胜到处走走转转,看到村里有的田地无人耕种,觉得"地荒着,难看"。2015 年,在当地扶贫干部的鼓励下,李德胜将乡亲们撂荒的稻田全部种起来,同时将进村道路两边的荒草杂灌进行了清理,修整了损毁的生产路,农忙时雇人插秧、收割,附近的村民和收割机师傅更愿意来了。在李德胜的精心打理下,当年就有了 2 万元的纯收入。

2016 年,更多的撂荒稻田被李德胜"征用",收入也水涨船高。

2017 年,光山县建立健全了"多彩田园"产业扶贫示范工程,正式形成了"多彩田园"产业扶贫整体框架,当年全县从事"多彩田园"产业的贫困户达到贫困户总数的 40%。村民们办起了家庭农场,种上了苗木花卉、有机稻,养起了山鸡黑猪和土鸭,还有稻虾共作和生态茶,到处是"房前屋后一亩茶,一塘肥鱼一群鸭"的场景。

脱贫后的李德胜干劲更大了,他把精力都花在 100 亩田地上。到 2019 年,李德胜当年的毛收入近 10 万元,刨去各项成本,纯收入超过 4 万元。

III. Implementing Fifteen Poverty Alleviation Action Plans

1. Poverty Alleviation through Industrial Development
【Case】Li Desheng and his 100 *mu* of "Colorful Farmland"

Li Desheng is a villager of Liwa villager group in Panlou Village, Mafan Town, Guangshan County in Xinyang.

For a variety of reasons, Li Desheng remained unmarried. Li began serving as the chief of the villager group in his twenties and since devoted himself to attending to village affairs and his farmland.

Since 2000, Li Desheng became the caregiver for the left-behind children in his extended family, taking care of the children of his brothers and nephews. For lack of stable source of income, Li Desheng was identified as an impoverished villager after the launch of the fight against poverty.

With the children under his care growing up and attending schools outside the village, Li Desheng became liberated from childcare. With little to occupy his time daily, Li Desheng began wandering around in the village. Upon seeing some farmlands left unattended, Li lamented "what a pitiful sight with so many fields left idle!" In 2015, Li Desheng, under the encouragement of poverty alleviation officials, undertook the cultivation of those unattended rice fields. Meanwhile, he offered to clear away the bushes and weeds along the flank of the main road and repair the crumbling road. During the busy farming seasons, he hired villagers to help with the sowing and harvesting. Seeing the opportunity to earn extra money, local villagers and harvester drivers were willing to pitch in when requested by Li Desheng. That year Li Desheng's hard work was amply rewarded, and he earned 20,000 *yuan* in net income.

In 2016, with more unattended rice fields taken over by him, Li Desheng reaped more money.

In 2017, with the "colorful farmland" demonstration project for poverty alleviation put in place, the general framework of poverty alleviation through industrial development featuring "colorful farmland" came into existence in Guangshan County. Consequently, the impoverished households involved in the

光山县"多彩田园"
"Colorful farmland" in Guangshan County

　　除了水稻，李德胜种的还有芝麻、黄豆、绿豆、玉米等小杂粮。这两年在种植水稻时，李德胜特意分出来一部分稻田，专门用于种植糯稻。他喜欢吃饭时喝点小酒，种点糯米，既能酿酒，天冷了又能打成糍粑，给亲朋好友送点。

　　光山糍粑有着1000多年的历史，甚至比光山县历史文化名人司马光的"年纪"还要大。前几年，光山县正式打出"光山十宝"的地方品牌，其中就有鸡公潭糍粑。"光山十宝"中的黑猪腊肉、咸麻鸭蛋、油挂面等原材料都来自"多彩田园"，加工生产带动了遍布全县的合作社、家庭农场，产品又通过"村淘"、电商企业流通到全国各地。在这个过程中，土地的直接产出增加了，农产品的附加值也增加了，生产销售环节都在

initiative of "colorful farmland" accounted for 40% of the overall impoverished households in the county. A large variety of family farms sprang up under this initiative, some cultivating trees, flowers and organic rice, some raising pheasants, black pigs and local ducks, some creatively raising shrimps in the rice fields, and some engaging in ecological tea cultivation. Everywhere presented a prosperous pastoral scene of "tea gardens in front of and behind the houses, fish and duck swimming together in ponds" in Guangshan County.

Lifted out of poverty, Li Desheng felt more motivated and spent all his time on the 100 mu of farmland. In 2019, Li Desheng earned 100,000 *yuan* in gross income and, after deducting costs, cashed in more than 40, 000 *yuan* in net income.

Apart from rice, Li Desheng also cultivated sesame and other coarse grain such as soybean, mung bean, and corn. In recent years, Li Desheng also cultivated a bit glutinous rice, which could be used to make glutinous rice wine, so that he could drink some at dinners. Meanwhile, this type of rice could also be used to make glutinous rice cake, being a perfect gift for friends and relatives.

Guangshan glutinous rice cake boasts a long history of more than 1,000 years, even older than the local historical celebrity Sima Guang (a household name in traditional Chinese legends). Several years ago, Guangshan County launched its local trademark products, collectively called "Ten Guangshan Treasures," in which Jigongtan glutinous rice cake was listed. Not only did the raw materials for such trademark products as black pig bacon, salted shelduck eggs and dried oil noodles come from "colorful farmland," the follow-up processing generated the emergence of agricultural cooperatives and family farms. Finally, their agricultural products were sold to many parts of the country through such platforms as village Taobao and E-commerce enterprises. Thanks to all this, the direct output of land and the added value of agricultural products have been sharply improved. Meanwhile, the production and sales of such products have generated an endless stream of jobs for villagers, and more impoverished households have been lifted out of poverty and become prosperous under this poverty alleviation framework.

不断创造就业机会，更多的贫困户通过自己的劳动摆脱贫困，走向小康。

【全景】发展产业是实现脱贫的根本之策

河南省把产业扶贫作为脱贫攻坚的主要方向，开展了"十大行动"：田园增收、养殖富民、旅游扶贫、电商扶贫、消费扶贫、致富带头人培育、新型经营主体提升、龙头企业带贫、金融扶贫、科技扶贫。

这些举措推动了河南扶贫产业的快速健康发展，增强了贫困群众的脱贫致富能力。

特色农业、小型加工业、乡村旅游业、电商产业、光伏产业等特色产业发展迅速，贫困人口的自我发展能力提高了。如全省旅游产业带贫人数 32 万余人，人均年增收 3500 元左右。

河南省有 475 万贫困人口通过产业帮扶增收脱贫，贫困地区农村居民人均可支配收入增速连续 8 年高于全省农村平均水平。全省 9536 个贫困村均有集体经济收入，其中收入 10 万～50 万元的占 52%，50 万元以上的有 201 个。

由于政策、资金、项目、人才、技术等资源要素向贫困地区集聚，一大批贫困县培育出了具有本地特色的扶贫产业，县域经济发展迅速。如淅川县依托南水北调水源地，探索出了"短中长"三线结合的产业发展路子，"短线"即发展食用菌、小龙虾、中药材等短平快项目，实现当年发展、当年见效、当年脱贫；"中线"即发展以软籽石榴、大樱桃、杏李为代表的生态林果，林下套种丹参、油牡丹、花生等经济作物，实现长短互补、以短养长；"长线"即依托良好的旅游资源和生态资源，重点发展生态旅游，保证群众当期能脱贫、远期能致富、未来可持续。

【Panorama】 Developing Industries Being Fundamental to Poverty Alleviation

With industrial development positioned as the primary strategy for poverty alleviation, ten initiatives have been launched in Henan Province, including raising villagers' income through family farms, enriching villagers through animal husbandry, poverty alleviation through tourism, poverty alleviation through E-commerce, poverty alleviation through consumption, cultivating role models to lead people toward prosperity, fostering new types of rural economic entity, poverty alleviation driven by leading enterprises, poverty alleviation through finance, and poverty alleviation through science and technology.

These initiatives have combined to promote the stable development of poverty alleviation and made the impoverished population better able to cast off poverty and become prosperous.

With the thriving of characteristic agriculture, small-scale processing, rural tourism, E-commerce industry and solar energy industry, many impoverished people are in a better position to seek self-development and improve their lives. For instance, more than 320,000 people in Henan have benefited from poverty alleviation through tourism, with an average of around 3,500 *yuan* added to their income annually.

In Henan, 4.75 million impoverished people have hitherto been lifted out of poverty and prospered through developing agricultural industries and the per capita disposable income for rural residents in the impoverished regions has witnessed a higher growth rate for 8 consecutive years than the provincial average in rural Henan. All the 9,536 impoverished villages in Henan have collective economic entities to benefit villagers, among which villages boasting the collective income between 100,000 *yuan* to 500,000 *yuan* account for 52% of the total and 201 villages have the collective income exceeding 500,000 *yuan*.

With favorable policies, funds, projects, talents, and technologies essential to poverty alleviation diverted to the impoverished regions, poverty alleviation industries with local characteristics have been cultivated in many impoverished counties in Henan, substantially boosting the local economic development in

清丰县刘张庄村的脱贫大棚
The vegetable greenhouses in Liuzhangzhuang Village, Qingfeng County

2. 就业创业扶贫

【故事】火红辣椒酱带来红火好日子

周秋耐是河南省许昌市襄城县范湖乡人。

1996年，周秋耐嫁到本乡铁炉陈村。婚后，小两口借钱购买了一辆小型拖拉机，干起了清运秸秆的营生。随着女儿、儿子的出生，秸秆清运生意难以为继，夫妻俩又琢磨起了家庭养羊项目，筹资购买40只羊羔儿，红红火火地干了起来。

these counties. Among them Xichuan County is a good case in point. Utilizing the geographical advantage of being the water source site for South-to-North Water Diversion Project, Xichuan County developed an integrated 3-dimensional industrial development model, combining "short-term, medium-term and long-term developments." "Short-term development" means focusing on projects that can generate immediate income within a short span, such as the cultivation of edible mushroom and medical herbs and raising lobsters, so that the impoverished people can get financial rewards immediately to cast off poverty within the year of their endeavor. "Medium-term development" features the complementary integration of the fruit tree planting, such as pomegranate, cherry, apricot and plum, with the cultivation of cash crops, including red-rooted salvia, oil peony and peanut, with cash crops planted under the fruit trees in the fields to make efficient use of the land. "Long-term development," in contrast, focuses on the development of ecological tourism to make full use of the local tourism and ecological resources in a bid to ensure that local people can eliminate poverty now, become wealthy in the near future, and retain their affluence in the long run.

2. Poverty Alleviation through Employment and Starting a Business
【Case】 The Red Chili Sauce Bringing about Affluent Lives

Zhou Qiunai is a female villager from Fanhu Town, Xiangcheng County, Xuchang of Henan Province.

In 1996, Zhou Qiunai married into Tiehchen Village from the same town. The new couple bought a tractor on loan and earned money through straw trucking. After the birth of their children, the family found itself unable to make a living depending on straw trucking and contemplated switching to raising sheep. They took out loans and scraped together enough money for a vigorous start by buying 40 lambs.

However, in 2003, the otherwise affluent family was plunged into misery when Zhou Qiunai's husband died a violent death. Faced with the heavy debt to repay and young mouths to feed, Zhou Qiunai found herself in distress with no way out.

Helplessly widowed, Zhou Qiunai had to juggle childcare and odd jobs. To scrape by she worked as a farm laborer picking chili and as a sales assistant in

2003年,周秋耐的丈夫因故去世,即将兴旺起来的幸福家庭支离破碎,面对沉重的债务、年幼的孩子,她的生活陷入困顿。

丈夫去世后,周秋耐一边照看孩子,一边在附近打零工,给别人摘过辣椒、当过超市售货员。这种生活状态持续数年,直到还清了数万元债务。

随着孩子长大上学,家庭开支越来越大,虽然乡、村两级干部给予了很多帮助,按政策给她的儿子办理了低保,但周秋耐认为一个家庭的幸福终究还要靠自己去奋斗。于是,她安排好孩子后,选择南下打工。然而,在南方务工期间,她患上了皮肤病,不得不辞职返乡。

2016年5月,周秋耐家被评定为范湖乡铁炉陈村建档立卡贫困户。襄城县税务局派驻铁路陈村第一书记张克强入户走访时,得知周秋耐掌握有酱菜制作技术,就鼓励她自主创业,并资助周秋耐外出学习培训。在大家的帮助下,周秋耐外出学习了辣椒酱、黄豆酱等酱菜的腌制技艺,对靠技术致富心里有了底儿。随后,她申请了小额扶贫贷款,联系购买了瓶子、封口机等生产设备。

2017年8月,周秋耐开始在家做起了辣酱生意,她坚持传统工艺,土法腌制,由于制作精细,物美价廉,逐步打开了周边乡村市场,先后参加了襄城县扶贫领域农产品电商交易会、第二届襄城首山油菜花节农产品展销会等,产品供不应求。

随后,驻村干部又协调周秋耐参加了电商培训,学习网上销售知识,她通过微信、抖音等网络平台推广、销售自己制作的酱菜,不但将小小的酱菜卖到了许昌、平顶山等地,还接到了来自省外的订单,把酱菜销售到了广东、安徽等省,产品销量也从最初的每月40多瓶到200多瓶,几个月下来出售的辣椒酱给周秋耐带来了两万多元的收入。2017年底,周秋耐家稳定脱贫。

虽然脱贫了,但周秋耐还有更大的理想,她要继续加油干,把传统

supermarkets. She had worked this way for several years until she finally could repay the family debt in the amount of tens of thousands of *yuan*.

While struggling hard to eke a living and pay for her children's education, Zhou Qiunai also received help from the local government and her sons were granted subsistence allowance. However, with her children growing up, the family expenses equally grew fast. Endeavoring to pursue happiness relying on hard work rather than outside help, she placed her children with her relatives and went to work in southern China for more money. However, after some time she had to quit and return home after being diagnosed with a skin disease.

In May, 2016, Zhou Qiunai was identified and registered as living in poverty by the local government. Then she received help from the First Secretary Zhang Keqiang, who was dispatched by the Tax Bureau of Xiangcheng County to take charge of poverty alleviation in the village. After discovering that Zhou Qiunai had a talent for pickle making, Zhang Keqiang encouraged her to start her small business. Funded by Zhang Keqiang and with the help from the local government, Zhou Qiunai went outside to receive systematic training in how to make preserved foods like chili sauce and soybean sauce. Feeling assured about making money depending on this specialized skill, Zhou Qiunai applied for a poverty alleviation microloan and purchased the necessary pickling equipment such as bottles and a sealing machine.

In August, 2017, Zhou Qiunai got the family workshop started selling sauces and her products were welcomed and eagerly purchased in the neighboring markets due to the traditional cooking technique, reasonable price, and delicious taste. She even went as far as attending Poverty Alleviation Agricultural Products E-commerce Trade Fair in Xiangcheng County and The Second Agricultural Products Fair of Oilseed Rape Flower Festival in Xiangcheng County, where her products were eagerly sought after.

Later, the village-based official for poverty alleviation arranged for Zhou Qiunai to receive E-commerce trainings to learn about online merchandising, paving the way for her to promote and sell her homemade pickle on such online platforms as WeChat and Tiktok. Amazingly she not only got the products sold to other cities of Henan, such as Xuchang and Pingdingshan, but also received orders from other provinces, such as Guangdong and Anhui. The monthly sales

的酱菜技艺传承下去，利用本地大面积种植辣椒的优势，带动村民们发展这项产业。

【全景】多种途径帮扶贫困劳动力就业创业

河南省帮助贫困劳动力就业创业，主要采用了六种就业途径：劳务协作输出就业、就地就近吸纳就业、居家灵活就业、自主创业带动就业、中介组织介绍就业、公益性岗位安置就业。

河南省先后开展了"雨露计划""春风行动""就业扶贫行动日""人力资源服务机构助力脱贫攻坚行动计划"等活动，掌握贫困劳动力就业动态，帮助就业不稳定的贫困劳动力上岗。

通过开展技能提升培训，提高贫困劳动力的就业能力。培训机构创新培训模式，开展种植、养殖、农产品加工、服装加工、家政服务等实用技能培训。如建成河南终身职业技能培训服务平台，建设38个贫困县劳动力转移就业品牌基地等。

群众在家门口的扶贫车间就业
A poverty alleviation workshop providing access to work near residents' homes

of her pickles surged from 40 bottles to over 200 bottles, earning Zhou over 20,000 *yuan* from the sales of chili sauce within the first few months of her pickle business. At the end of 2017, Zhou Qiunai was identified as having eliminated poverty.

Not content with all this success, the aspiring Zhou Qiunai aimed higher. Intending to promote the traditional pickle making technique and take full advantage of the large-scale planting of chili in her hometown, she generously helped the fellow villagers to engage in and promote pickle making to achieve common prosperity.

【Panorama】 Helping the Impoverished Get Employment and Start a Business through Multiple Means

In general, six means have been adopted in Henan Province to help the impoverished get employment and start a business: employment through coordinated labor export, creating job vacancies in the locality, home-based flexible employment, creating jobs through starting a business, employment through the recommendation of job service agency and employment in the public welfare posts.

To foster employment, a series of initiatives, namely the "rain and dew plan," "spring breeze action," "employment and poverty alleviation day," and "assistance program for the fight against poverty by the human resources and job service agencies," have been launched to keep track of the employment status of the impoverished and assist the impoverished people facing unstable employment in finding better work.

Additionally, vocational training sessions have been organized to help the impoverished become more employable. A wide range of subjects involving practical skills, such as planting, breeding, processing of agricultural products, garment making and housekeeping, have been incorporated into the training program. Meanwhile, some innovative training patterns have also been adopted. For example, Henan provincial lifelong vocational training platform has been launched and 38 employment bases for labor transfer in the impoverished counties have been established.

Additional support has been rendered to migrants returning home

加大返乡创业扶持力度，带动贫困劳动力家门口就业。通过政策推动、园区带动、项目驱动，鼓励更多"能人"返乡下乡创业，发挥创业带贫效应。如成立"河南省农民工返乡创业投资基金"，为返乡农民工发放创业担保贷款。

开发公益性岗位，确保贫困劳动力就业底线。河南省先后出台《河南省公益性岗位管理办法》等，制定各类公益性岗位管理规范，提升乡村公益性岗位保障水平。

3. 生态扶贫

【故事】田铺大塆留住美丽乡愁

位于大别山区的河南省新县田铺乡有个田铺大塆，村落房屋始建于明末清初，距今400余年。这里有江南水乡的灵秀，豫南乡土的韵味。然而，田铺大塆村民一度守着绿水青山，却找不到饭碗。

韩光莹家世代居住在田铺大塆。20世纪90年代，找不到挣钱门路的韩光莹开始外出打工，家里一天比一天空落，老宅也年久失修。

改变悄然而至。2014年，田铺大塆成功入选第三批中国传统村落名录。随后，新县规划"九镇十八湾"，发展全域旅游。田铺大塆的基础设施、公共服务和居住环境得到综合整治，人工湿地、大塘花田面目一新，原始风貌应留尽留。远在韩国的韩光莹一直关注着家乡的变化，2016年他辞掉工作，回到老家。

在政府的帮助下，韩光莹投入20多万元，将自家旧宅进行改造，开办了全村第一家民宿店，起名"老家寒舍"。"老家寒舍"门口有竹、门头挂匾、院里种花，淳朴中透着高雅，吸引了很多游客，年收入十多万元。

"老家寒舍"的成功示范，让村民们放开了手脚，村里相继建起十多家民宿。韩光莹牵头成立民宿合作社，建了民宿接待中心，规范经营，

for business startups in order to create more jobs in the local area for the impoverished. Through the provision of favorable policies, startup hubs and startup projects, growing numbers of aspiring and competent people have been motivated to start their businesses in their hometown to lead more impoverished people out of poverty. For instance, the investment fund for business startups of the returnee migrant workers has been launched to provide secured business startup loans for them.

More public welfare posts have been provided and created to guarantee the employment threshold for the impoverished population. Henan provincial government has issued *The Regulation for the Public Welfare Posts in Henan* to standardize the administration of public welfare posts and improve the welfare for people working in public welfare posts in rural areas.

3. Poverty Alleviation through Ecological Conservation
【Case】The Traditional Village of Tianpudawan Retaining the Sweet Nostalgia

The traditional village of Tianpudawan, located in the Dabie Mountain area in Tianpu Town, Xinxian County of Henan, dates back to the transitional period between the Ming and Qing dynasties, and boasts a history of more than 400 years. The local landscape is characterized by the exquisite watery charm of southern China and the rural pastoral beauty typical in southern Henan. Despite being blessed with the lucid water and lush mountains, the villagers here were once unable to find jobs to support themselves.

Han Guangying and his family lived in Tianpudawan Village for generations. As early as in the 1990s, Han Guangying, unable to find jobs to earn money in his hometown, went out to find job opportunities, leaving the family house unattended and run-down.

In 2014, with Tianpudawan Village included on the List of Traditional Chinese Villages (the third batch), change has crept in for the village. The local government of Xinxian County launched the tourism blueprint of "nine towns and eighteen bays" to promote the local tourism. Subsequently, with the improvement in infrastructure, public services, living environment, and the emergence of constructed wetland, fish ponds and flower gardens, the village has taken on a

统一管理,携手共赢。

韩光莹的二嫂曾祥英瞅准商机,开了一家"英子饭店"。每逢节假日,曾祥英的饭店客源不断,一天能挣2000多元。由于人手不够,曾祥英的女儿也从外地回了家,一起创业。

韩光莹大哥韩光志开的民宿店紧靠池塘,推窗见水,远望见绿。坐在阳台上,摆一壶茶,拉几段二胡,练几幅书法,甚至发一会儿呆,都是享受。因为山美水美,许多摄影师走进田铺大塆,流连忘返。日子久了,韩光志家成了"摄影师之家"。从迎春花开,到桃花开、樱花开……一年四季,摄影师扛着器材,拍累了,休息两天,找朋友,晒晒照片。韩光志坐在一旁,悠悠闲闲就能赚钱。

不只是韩家,卖手绣鞋垫的"匠艺工坊"、卖竹编的"不秋草"店、卖蜂蜜和豆腐乳等土特产品的"田铺伴手礼"店,20多家小店就地取材,各具特色。这些小店租用了几十套院子,租金直接带给村民收益,还解决了几十名村民的就业问题。

田铺大塆(新华社)
Tianpudawan Village (the Xinhua News Agency)

new look while preserving its traditional rural flavor. Closely keeping track of the overwhelming changes in his hometown while working in South Korea, in 2016 Han Guangying made a bold decision: quitting his job and returning home.

With the help from the local government, Han Guangying invested more than 200,000 *yuan* in the renovation of his family house and transformed it into a homestay hotel, the first of its kind in the village, naming it "Laojia Hanshe" (meaning a home-like hotel for nostalgic guests). With bamboo trees planted at the gate, inscribed plaques placed above the doors and fragrant flowers dotting the yard, the homestay hotel combined tranquil plainness with exquisite elegance to attract streams of visitors and reaped more than 100,000 *yuan* in annual income for Han Guangying.

Seeing the popularity and success of "Laojia Hanshe," other villagers began to follow Han's lead and soon more than ten homestay hotels sprang up in the village. Afterwards, under Han Guangying's initiative and coordination, a homestay cooperative and a homestay reception center were subsequently established to provide standardized service and regulate the homestay management to achieve win-win results.

Zeng Xiangying, Han Guangying's second sister-in-law, also grasped a business opportunity and opened a restaurant named "Yingzi Restaurant." With tourists flocking in during weekends and holidays, her restaurant remained busy, earning more than 2,000 *yuan* daily. Shorthanded, Zeng Xiangying encouraged her daughter to come home to join the family business.

Han Guangzhi, Han Guangying's eldest brother, ran a homestay hotel close to a pond that offered guests an up-close water view through the window and a view of the distant green hills. Sitting on the balcony, homestay guests can sip tea, play the Erhu (a traditional Chinese musical instrument), practice calligraphy or just indulge in moments of idleness. Beckoned by the picturesque rural landscape, many photographers came and lingered on for days in Tianpudawan Village, turning Han Guangzhi's home into "a home for photographers." With the blooming of winter jasmine, peach, cherry, and other flowers coming one after the other around the year, flocks of photographers were attracted to the village. Here in the village, they strolled about, took photos, rested for a while, chatted with friends, and showed off their photos proudly, indulging in the simple happiness.

2019年9月16日,习近平总书记来这里考察调研,他走进一家家小店,与百姓手拉手、唠家常、问冷暖。他说,发展乡村旅游不要搞大拆大建,要因地制宜、因势利导,把传统村落改造好、保护好。

2019年,田铺大塆启用游客集散中心,采取"创客+公司+合作社+农户"的旅游经营模式,完成村庄亮化绿化工程和旅游标准化建设。当年,田铺大塆接待游客100余万人次,旅游综合收入达8500余万元。

【全景】做好生态扶贫四项重要工作

河南省重视贫困地区的生态扶贫,主要做好四个方面的工作。

加大对贫困地区的资金支持力度,进行生态补偿扶持。争取国家生态护林员补助资金,落实退耕还林补助资金、公益林生态效益补偿资金,创新建立宅基地复垦券制度,将贫困地区复垦的建设用地指标在全省范围内交易,为贫困地区筹集资金。全省聘任建档立卡贫困户护林员4.2万人,带动12万贫困人口增收。

进行生态工程建设,改善贫困地区生态环境。开展"森林河南"建设,加快推进沿黄湿地公园、伏牛山植物大观园等国土绿化及生态修复工程,直接带动10余万贫困人口就业。每年依托森林旅游收入达160亿元,惠及5万个贫困家庭。

治理生态环境,提升贫困地区生态品质。通过整治农村环境,治理水土流失,防治大气、水、土壤污染,改善贫困地区人居环境。2017年以来累计筹措水土保持补助资金9.4亿元,新增水土流失防治面积475平方千米。

发展生态产业,促进贫困地区高质量发展。推广"企业+专业合作组织+基地+农户"模式,发展林下经济、森林康养、林果加工等产业,贫困地区实现了"生态保护、环境美化、群众增收、区域发展"。2017年以来,全省220家林业龙头企业带动贫困户5.5万户、12.61万人就业,人均年增收3650元。

Meanwhile, Han Guangzhi, the homestay owner, also enjoyed himself, remaining at home and making money simultaneously.

In addition to Han Guangying's extended family, other villagers also set up their own home-based business with distinctive local features, ranging from "Jiangyi Gongfang" selling embroidered insoles and "Buqiucao" selling bamboo-weaved products, to gift shops selling honey, fermented bean curd and other local specialties. There were more than 20 shops of this kind in the village, each making the best use of local resources and traditional handicrafts. Some shops were in the rented family yards of villagers, directly adding to villagers' income and creating jobs for dozens of villagers as well.

On September 16, 2019, on his inspection visit to Tianpudawan Village, President Xi Jinping walked into these shops and chatted cordially with villagers, shaking hands with them and asking about their daily lives and business. He remarked that rural tourism should be pursued according to and taking full advantage of the local conditions rather than engaging in large-scale demolition and reconstruction to better preserve and protect traditional villages.

In 2019, when the Tianpudawan tourist center was established, a new tourism management model, namely the "makers plus enterprises plus tourism collectives plus farmers" model, emerged to coordinate the tourism development in the village. Under this initiative, the village has become greener and brighter, and tourism service has been standardized. In that year, Tianpudawan Village received more than one million visitors and brought in 85 million *yuan* in overall tourism income.

【Panorama】 Implementing Four Imperatives in Poverty Alleviation through Ecological Conservation

The governments at all levels in Henan have attached great importance to poverty alleviation through ecological conservation in the impoverished regions, mainly focusing on efforts in four aspects.

More poverty alleviation financial support has been diverted to the impoverished regions for ecological compensation. Subsidy for the national ecological forest rangers has been filed for, and the subsidy for returning farmland to forests and the ecological compensation fund for public welfare forests have

黄河大堤范县段

The Yellow River dike in Fanxian County

4. 金融扶贫

【故事】解锁脱贫攻坚的金融"密码"

地处豫晋陕三省接合部的河南省三门峡市卢氏县，因"八山一水一分田"的特殊地貌，一度成为河南贫困发生率最高、贫困程度最深的县。

万小劳是卢氏县范里镇碾子沟村人，因为身体有残疾再加上投资失败，40多岁的他是村里多年的贫困户。

2016年，中国联通河南分公司对当地进行对口帮扶。碾子沟村由于海拔高，种植的玉米生长周期长，玉米糁的黏度和营养价值更高，口感也比普通玉米好。碾子沟村委会投资1万元购买了玉米糁加工机械，并以每年1000元的价格租赁给万小劳，帮助其开展玉米糁加工业务。

been duly granted. An innovative homestead reclamation voucher mechanism has been initiated and the quota of construction land for reclamation in the impoverished regions has been allowed to be freely transferred within Henan Province to raise money for the impoverished regions. More than 42,000 people from the registered impoverished households have been hired to work as forest rangers, financially benefiting around 120,000 impoverished people.

Ecological projects have been vigorously launched to improve the ecological environment in the impoverished regions. In Henan "adding forests to Henan action" has been implemented and the greening and ecological renovation projects, such as the Wetland Parks along the Yellow River and the Funiu Mountain Plantation Garden, have been stepped up, directly generating jobs for more than 100,000 impoverished people. The annual forest-related tourism revenue in Henan has risen to around 16 billion yuan, benefiting 50,000 impoverished households.

Ecological problems have been addressed to upgrade the ecosystem in the impoverished regions. To improve the rural environment, a series of measures have been adopted, aiming at the prevention and control of soil erosion as well as air, water, and soil pollution, and consequently the living conditions in the impoverished regions have been considerably improved. Since 2017, a total of 940 million yuan has been allocated to subsidize the conservation of soil and water, and 475 square kilometers of land has been newly incorporated into the scheme for prevention and control of water and soil erosion.

Ecological industries have been developed to promote the high-quality development in the impoverished regions. The new business model of "enterprises plus agricultural collectives plus agricultural bases plus farmers" has been widely promoted and new industries such as under-forest economy, forest therapy and fruit processing have been vigorously developed. These measures have been combined to bring about improved ecological conservation, a more beautiful rural environment, higher incomes for farmers, and a more vigorous regional development in the impoverished regions. Since 2017, more than 220 leading forestry enterprises have rendered assistance to 55,000 impoverished households and provided jobs for 126,100 people, with the average annual income per person being raised by 3,650 yuan.

通过金融扶贫，万小劳拿到了5万元免息贷款。有了这5万元的免息贷款，2018年春节前，万小劳20天打出了两万斤玉米糁，实现毛利润6万多元。

万小劳在玉米糁加工之外，还养了9头黑猪，因为玉米糁的副产品麸皮是养猪的绝佳原材料。

在距离碾子沟村18公里的卢氏县范里镇苏村，30多岁的李章文与万小劳不同，他年富力强、踏实肯干，但由于缺技术、少资金，始终摸不到致富门路，也成了村里的贫困户。

一筹莫展之际，脱贫攻坚战打响了，李章文在政府扶持下，学会了种植香菇。2017年，卢氏开展金融扶贫，他申请到5万元免息贷款。正是这5万元的免息贷款，帮助李章文租到了4个香菇大棚并赊销了4万多棒香菇菌种，当年毛收入近9万元。因为李章文是文明诚信户，2018年，李章文利用免息贷款扩大了香菇大棚的生产规模，自己也成功脱贫。

万小劳和李章文的脱贫得益于卢氏县的金融扶贫政策。

2017年初，在河南省政府的直接推动下，卢氏金融扶贫试点工作开始启动，在省市县三级联动和金融等相关部门多方参与下，按照"政银联动、风险共担、多方参与、合作共赢"的工作思路，通过构建"金融服务、信用评价、风险防控、产业支撑"四大体系，形成了金融扶贫"卢氏模式"。

"卢氏模式"的深入实施，极大促进了卢氏县域经济的发展。到2020年7月，卢氏县广大农户通过扶贫小额贷款或惠农普惠贷款的支持，有效解决了发展生产、在家就业的融资需求，全县发展香菇2.3亿袋、烟叶7万亩，种植丹参、苍术、黄精、黄芩等中药材3.6万亩，栽植优生连翘6.2万亩……

4. Poverty Alleviation through Finance
【Case】 Deciphering the Financial Key to Poverty Elimination

Lying at the junction of the three provinces of Henan, Shanxi and Shaanxi, Lushi County in Sanmenxia in western Henan has unique geographical features, with 80% of the terrain being hills, 10% covered by water and another 10% being farmland. Due to the unfavorable natural environment, Lushi County was once the most impoverished county with the highest incidence of poverty in Henan Province.

Wan Xiaolao, a villager in his forties from Nianzigou Village, Fanli Town in Lushi County, suffered physical disability and investment failure, and remained registered as impoverished for many years.

In 2016, the Henan Branch of China Unicom started to undertake the targeted poverty alleviation in Nianzigou Village. Due to the high altitude of the village and longer growth cycle of corn there, corn grits produced in the village boast higher viscosity, higher nutritional value and better taste than those produced anywhere else. The village committee invested 10,000 yuan to purchase the machinery for corn grits processing and rented it to Wan Xiaolao on a yearly rent of 1,000 yuan to assist him with business startup costs.

Under the scheme of poverty alleviation through finance, Wan Xiaolao received a 50,000 yuan interest-free loan. Wan Xiaolao used this investment to expand the business and yielded 10,000 kilograms of corn grits only within 20 days before the Spring Festival of 2018, grossing more than 60,000 yuan.

Apart from engaging in corn grits processing, Wan Xiaolao raised 9 black pigs to earn extra money as the byproducts in corn grits processing are perfect feed for pigs.

Eighteen kilometers away from Nianzigou Village was the Village of Sucun in Fanli Town of Lushi County. Li Zhangwen, a villager in his thirties, had a different story from Wan Xiaolao's. Young, strong-bodied, diligent and down-to-earth as he was, his lack of specialized skill and investment money held him back and he was also registered as impoverished.

Opportunity knocked for Li Zhangwen after the launch of the fight against poverty by Chinese government. With the help and guidance of the local

【全景】金融扶贫给予贫困户特惠倾斜

"卢氏模式"是河南金融扶贫的创新和实践,这一模式在河南复制、在全国推广,受到了中共中央领导的批示肯定,写入了河南省委、省政府的纲领性文件。金融扶贫"卢氏模式"荣获"全球减贫案例有奖征集活动"最佳减贫案例。

"卢氏模式"在全省推广后,形成了覆盖全省农村地区的县乡村三级金融服务网络。河南推进精准扶贫企业贷款,支持企业带动建档立卡贫困户发展,通过"公司+贫困户""公司+基地+贫困户"等方式,将贫困户纳入现代产业发展体系。至 2020 年底,全省累计发放精准扶贫企业贷款 164.53 亿元,支持带贫企业 2317 家,带贫 26.49 万户。

办理扶贫贷款
A poverty alleviation loan is being processed.

全省组织各家金融机构,在贷款规模、贷款利率、审批效率等方面给予贫困群众特惠倾斜。不断扩大金融支持服务面,将贫困户扶贫小额信贷政策支持范围扩大到边缘户;扩大对一般农户、中小微企业、个体

government, Li received training in mushroom farming. In 2017, when the initiative of poverty alleviation through finance was launched in Lushi County, he obtained an interest-free loan in the amount of 50,000 yuan. Using this investment, Li rented 4 mushroom greenhouses and purchased 40,000 mushroom spawns on credit, enabling him to gross almost 90,000 yuan that year alone. On account of his sound credibility, Li obtained another interest-free loan in 2018 and scaled up mushroom production, finally allowing him to eliminate poverty.

The successful elimination of poverty for Wan Xiaolao and Li Zhangwen can be credited to the initiative of poverty alleviation through finance in Lushi County.

In early 2017, under the guidance from Henan provincial government, Lushi County launched a pilot project of poverty alleviation through finance. With the coordinated efforts of governments at provincial, municipal and county levels and active participation of relevant financial departments, an integrated system of poverty alleviation through finance was founded in Lushi County, combining financial service, credit evaluation, risk control and industrial support, and was dubbed "the Lushi model of poverty alleviation." This model featured government-bank coordination, risks sharing, multiple participation of all sectors and win-win results, and achieved remarkable results.

Since the further implementation of the Lushi model of poverty alleviation, the economic development in the county has been greatly spurred. By July, 2020, many farmers had enjoyed financial support in the form of poverty alleviation microloan or inclusive financial loan to fund their business startups and home-based business, and the financial support had generated astonishing results, producing 230 million bags of mushroom, 70,000 *mu* of leaf tobacco, 36,000 *mu* of land devoted to planting medical herbs, such as red-rooted salvia, rhizome of Chinese atractylodes, sealwort, skullcap, etc., and 62,000 *mu* of high-quality forsythia.

【Panorama】Poverty Alleviation through Finance Giving Preferential Treatment to the Impoverished Households

The Lushi model of poverty alleviation emerged as the innovative implementation of poverty alleviation through finance in Henan. The model has

工商户和农业经营主体等群体的贷款覆盖面。至 2020 年底，全省累计发放扶贫小额贷款 615.32 亿元，惠及 146.43 万户贫困户。

5. 健康扶贫

【故事】健康帮扶让贫困户绽笑颜

2020 年金秋十月，驻马店平舆县庙湾镇贫困户李新妹自家小院迎来了一年中最美的时光。小花圃里，花儿开得正艳，一株株绿植枝繁叶茂，充满生机与希望。"听说俺县脱贫攻坚获得了中国大奖，俺这心里乐呵啊。"正在打扫庭院的李新妹说。

2019 年 10 月 17 日，在全国脱贫攻坚奖表彰大会暨先进事迹报告会上，平舆县实践探索出的"互联网 + 分级诊疗 + 家庭签约医生"健康扶贫模式，荣获中国脱贫攻坚"组织创新奖"。

"老百姓足不出村也能享受优质的诊疗服务，危急时刻为抢救病人赢取了宝贵的时间。"李新妹对此深有感触。

2017 年 11 月，李新妹突发肺源性心脏病，病情十分危急，由于地处偏远，急救车无法及时赶到，村卫生室当即通过平台联通县医院专家，会诊病情，指导用药治疗，赢取了宝贵的抢救时间，最终李新妹转危为安。

在平舆县和李新妹一样尝到健康帮扶甜头的还有很多家庭。

59 岁的老王岗乡甘港村村民郭小多，13 岁患上化脓性骨髓炎，一年后股骨头坏死，成天疼得睡不着觉。

2016 年 5 月，郭小多被识别为贫困户。从此，他再也不用为每年高昂的医药费而发愁。让郭小多没有想到的是，平舆县实施"三级诊疗"后，看病不用花钱，村医胡长征隔三差五地到他家中做基础检查，乡卫生院医生王俊丽定期进行健康指导，县人民医院医生胡新房经常带着先进的医疗设备上门诊疗……这一系列的健康帮扶给郭小多带来了新希望。

在扶贫干部群众的共同帮助下，郭小多病情逐渐好转。紧接着，郭

been adopted in other parts of Henan and promoted nationwide. It was approved and acclaimed by high-level leaders of the Communist Party of China and was included as a key strategy in the guideline documents of CPC Henan provincial committee and Henan provincial government. The Lushi model of poverty alleviation through finance was selected as the best poverty reduction case in "Global Solicitation on Poverty Reduction Practices."

The subsequent promotion of "the Lushi model" in Henan has brought into being a three-tier financial service network at county, town and village levels, benefiting all the rural areas in the province. Through granting loans to enterprises engaging in targeted poverty alleviation, encouraging enterprise-driven poverty alleviation of the registered impoverished households and adopting the innovative models of "enterprises plus impoverished households" or "enterprises plus agricultural base plus impoverished households" in poverty alleviation, the impoverished households have been incorporated into the modern industrial development scheme by the government. By the end of 2020, a total of 16.453 billion yuan in targeted poverty alleviation loans had been granted to enterprises, rendering financial support to 2,317 enterprises engaging in poverty alleviation and aiding 264,900 impoverished households.

Preferential treatment in the size and interest of loans and loan approval time has been given to the impoverished population from all the financial institutions in Henan. The range of financial support has been steadily expanded and poverty alleviation microloan for the impoverished households has been extended to benefit households that are vulnerable to impoverishment. Efforts have also been made to extend the loan coverage to benefit general farmers, micro-, small and medium enterprises, individual business owners and agricultural business entities. By the end of 2020, poverty alleviation microloans totaling 61.532 billion yuan had been issued in Henan, benefiting 1,464,300 impoverished households.

5. Poverty Alleviation through Healthcare Assistance

【Case】 Healthcare Support Restoring Smiles to the Impoverished Households

One October day in 2020, Li Xinmei, an impoverished villager from Miaowan Town, Pingyu County of Zhumadian, was cleaning her courtyard,

小多拄着双拐在村里开起了代销铺，2017年摘掉了贫困户的帽子。

如今，郭小多没了生活和心理上的负担，闲暇之余，家中不大的院子里种满了花花草草，郭小多也把满满的幸福写上了笑脸。

从2016年到2019年，平舆县推行实施了村、乡、县互联网诊疗平台、县域内就诊一卡通，建立了居民电子健康档案数据库、慢性病人群数据库等健康保障体系，通过远程会诊、远程检验、远程教学、康复指导等医疗服务，聚合了优质医疗资源，实现线上线下全程高效对接，创造出健康扶贫的"平舆速度、平舆力度、平舆温度"。

【全景】基本实现"小病不出村，大病不出县"

河南省实施健康扶贫工程以来，解决了群众因病致贫、因病返贫等问题，百姓得到了实惠。

河南省卫生健康委作为健康扶贫牵头部门，千方百计落实贫困人口基本医疗有保障。对全省139个县、2000多个乡镇、61万因病致贫户摸底核查，建立了因病致贫、因病返贫人口动态管理数据库。在摸清底数的基础上，研究制定全省健康扶贫专项工作方案，确保贫困人口"看得起病、看得好病、方便看病、少生病"。

"互联网＋健康扶贫"的三级医疗服务体系，让群众享受到了优质医疗资源，常见病在村镇里就能看好，避免了就医的奔波之苦，又降低了外出看病的费用。

which was alive with blooming flowers and lush plants in the flower garden. When seeing us, she exclaimed joyfully, "How happy I am when I know our county has won a national award for poverty alleviation efforts!"

On October 17, 2019, a national commendation conference was held on which individuals and institutions were commended for their outstanding work in poverty alleviation and were invited to deliver reports on their work. The Pingyu model of poverty alleviation through healthcare assistance, namely the "Internet plus tiered diagnosis and treatment plus contractual family doctor" model, won the national "Organizational Innovation Award" for its success in poverty alleviation.

Li Xinmei added, "Thanks to all this, we villagers can have access to high-quality diagnosis and treatment without leaving the village and it can save a lot of time for saving the lives of the critically ill."

In October, 2017, Li Xinmei had a sudden heart attack caused by critical pulmonary heart disease. As her village was too remote for an ambulance visit, the village doctor immediately contacted a specialist from the county-level hospital online for remote diagnosis and treatment, gaining the precious time in saving her life. Thanks to the timely medical treatment, Li Xinmei pulled through.

Apart from Li Xinmei, there were many other families in Pingyu County benefiting from this healthcare assistance system.

Guo Xiaoduo, a 59-year-old villager from Gan'gang Village of Laowanggang Town, was diagnosed with pyogenic ostcomyclitis at the age of 13, but one year later it developed into osteonecrosis of femoral head, giving him constant pain and depriving him of sleep.

In May, 2016, Guo Xiaoduo was identified as impoverished and was soon relieved from worry about his high medical expenses. Much to his joyful surprise, the three-tiered diagnosis and treatment system adopted in Pingyu County enabled him to spend comparatively little on medical treatment. Meanwhile, with Hu Changzheng, the village doctor, paying regular visits for basic medical checks, Wang Junli, the doctor from township health center, dispensing regular health advice and Hu Xinfang, the doctor from the county hospital, making frequent house calls with advanced medical equipment, all these healthcare assistances restored hope to the once desperate invalid.

Guo Xiaoduo gradually recovered with the joint help from the village-baed

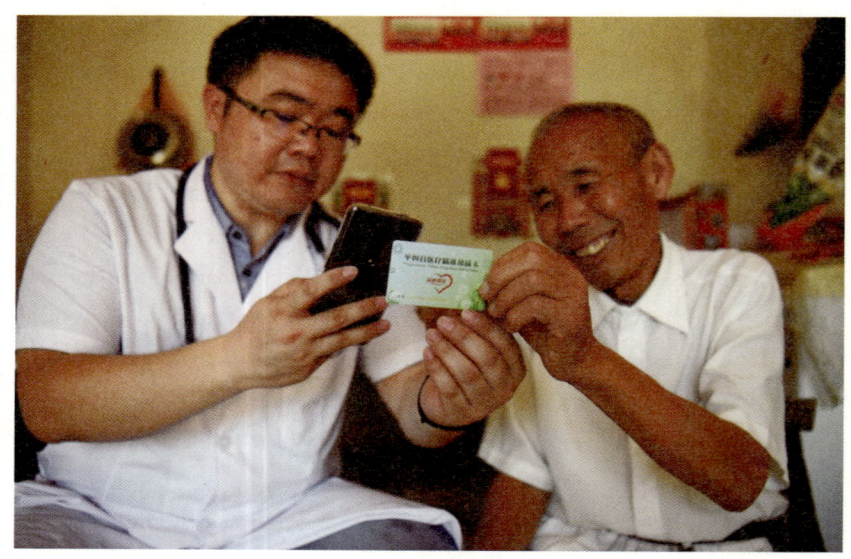

诊疗信息联网
Diagnostic and therapeutic information in an all-in-one medical card

全省各地建立的医疗保障和救助工作体系独具特色，它将建档立卡贫困人口全部纳入基本医保和医疗救助范围，全省贫困人口看病就医自付费用比例降低到10%以内。

到2020年底，河南省累计救治大病患者14.4万人次，使贫困家庭患者得到最大程度救治，降低贫困人口的就医负担，做到不落一人；对487万贫困人口开展家庭医生签约服务，实现远程医疗覆盖所有贫困县、贫困村卫生室，贫困地区乡镇卫生院全部具备50种以上常见病诊治能力，县域内就诊率达95%以上，基本实现小病不用出村，大病不用出县。

poverty alleviation officials and fellow villagers. Later, he bought crutches to help him move around and ran a consignment shop in the village, eventually finding himself off the impoverished list by 2017.

Now Guo Xiaoduo, free from financial worry, wears a broad smile every day and attends to the flowers and plants in his courtyard in his spare time. He has been totally transformed into a happy man.

Between 2016 and 2019, Pingyu County launched an Internet-based diagnosis and treatment platform, integrating medical institutions at village, town and county levels, and the countywide all-in-one medical card system. A digital personal health record database and database for the chronically ill were also launched. With the implementation of remote diagnosis, remote treatment, remote teaching and rehabilitation counseling, quality medical resources were fully tapped to achieve the integration of online and offline medical resources, generating a new model of poverty alleviation through healthcare assistance featuring efficiency, broad coverage, and humanistic care.

【Panorama】 Virtually Achieving Medical Treatment of Minor Ailments within the Village and of Critical Diseases within the County

Following the implementation of poverty alleviation through healthcare assistance, the danger of sinking into poverty and slipping back into poverty due to diseases among residents in Henan has been effectively avoided, substantially benefiting this particularly vulnerable population.

Henan Provincial Health Commission, as the primary coordinator for the poverty alleviation through healthcare assistance initiative, has adopted a multitude of measures to ensure the impoverished population's access to basic medical services. Following thorough investigation and verification of 610,000 households falling into poverty due to diseases in 2,000-plus towns of 139 counties, Henan has launched a dynamic management database, targeting those at risk of falling back into poverty from disease. With the data accurately collected, a provincial action plan for poverty alleviation through healthcare assistance has been formulated to ensure that the impoverished population can afford medical expenses, receive adequate medical treatment, have convenient access to medical services, and become less prone to disease.

6. 教育扶贫

【故事】求学路上展"笑颜"

"凯旋""笑颜",这两个好听的名字表达了父母对孩子未来的美好期望和虔诚祝福,但是郸城县汲水乡的李凯旋和李笑颜姐妹俩,童年并不快乐和幸福。

2014年,姐妹俩的父亲因意外去世,家中的"顶梁柱"轰然倒塌,原本幸福的家庭顿时失去了依靠。母亲路思兰一人拉扯姐妹俩艰难度日,生活的压力让这个家庭一度喘不过气来。当年,14岁的李凯旋正读九年级,姐姐李笑颜正读高中。穷人的孩子早当家,懂事的李凯旋为了减轻家庭经济负担,打算放弃上学而出去打工挣钱。

2017年,郸城县率先在周口市实行"教育村长"制度,聘任3171名有担当、能奉献、熟悉村情的"教育村长"和万千教师深入农户家庭,宣传教育扶贫政策,了解民情、学情,排查辍学情况,群众的所有"教育事"都能得到及时解决,所有困难学生都能及时得到精准资助。

"教育村长"刘桂荣在走访时,得知李凯旋的情况后,对她说:"你不能辍学,读书才是希望和出路,才能改变家庭命运,学校学习和生活费用由我负责协调。"第二天,刘桂荣就把3000元钱送到李凯旋家中,并坚持每月为她捐助生活费500元。

在刘桂荣的帮扶下,教育资助、低保、企业带贫等扶贫政策一一得到落实,不但减免了姐妹俩的学费,还给予了助学补助、低保金和带贫资金,同时,学校还安排路思兰当上了寝室管理员,这样,一家人的生活终于有了着落,不再为没钱上学而发愁。

2018年,李凯旋以优异的成绩被清华大学录取,李笑颜也考取了心仪的大学。进入大学后,姐妹俩继续享受着教育扶贫政策的帮扶,每个学期都能拿到特困救助资金,特别是李凯旋还享受到学校的"奖、助、贷、勤、免、补"全方位资助,同时,姐妹俩也得到了社会各界爱心人士的无私捐助。

The three-tiered medical service system integrating Internet with poverty alleviation through healthcare assistance has guaranteed people's access to high-quality medical resources so that some common ailments can be treated within villages or towns, saving patients from making long-distance trips for medical treatment and bringing down the expenses when seeking treatment elsewhere.

With the emergence of distinctive healthcare guarantee and assistance systems in different regions of Henan, the impoverished population was incorporated into the basic medical insurance and medical assistance framework. As a result, expenses paid by the impoverished population for medical treatment have been lowered to less than 10% of the total cost for treatment.

By the end of 2020, an aggregated total of 144,000 patients with critical conditions had received medical treatment, rendering the utmost treatment to patients from the impoverished families and alleviating their financial burden from medical treatment with no one left behind. A total of 4.87 million impoverished people gained access to contractual family doctor services and remote medical services were made accessible to all the village clinics in the impoverished villages and counties. All township health centers in the impoverished regions in Henan developed diagnosis and treatment capacity for 50-plus common diseases. The hospital visit rate within counties had reached more than 95%, ensuring medical treatment of minor ailments within the village and of critical diseases within the county.

6. Poverty Alleviation through Education

【Case】 "Broad Smiles" from Two Girls in Their Pursuit of Education

The two pleasant names "Kaixuan" (victorious return) and "Xiaoyan" (broad smiles) were given to two sisters from a rural family in Jishui Town, Dancheng County. The names vividly conveyed the great hope and sincere blessing from their parents. However, the two girls were not blessed with a happy childhood.

In 2014, tragedy struck the two girls' family when their father died in an accident, leaving the otherwise happy family deprived of the backbone breadwinner and plunging the family into helplessness. Their mother, Lu Silan, struggled to raise the two girls alone and the family lived a miserable life under overwhelming financial stress. That year the 14-year-old Li Kaixuan was a ninth

一路走来，受到资助的姐妹俩很懂得感恩，主动加入学校的志愿服务队当中，常参加各项公益活动，尽已所能回报社会。

【全景】确保每个孩子不因贫困失学辍学

河南教育扶贫以"义务教育有保障"为核心，落实"保障学业、支持事业、促进就业、助推产业"，让贫困家庭的孩子接受良好的教育，是阻断贫困代际传递的治本之策。

河南教育扶贫的主要内容有：完善从全学段贫困家庭学生资助政策，改善贫困地区办学条件和硬件建设，加强贫困地区农村教师队伍建设，支持贫困县中职学校开展专业实训基地和信息化建设，发挥高校优势助推贫困地区的产业发展等。

2016年以来，河南省累计资助建档立卡家庭义务教育阶段学生522.42万人次，发放资助金38.16亿元；新建改扩建中小学、幼儿园2.25万所；先后为贫困地区招聘特岗教师3.72万名；举办职业教育精准脱贫技能培训班，对3.82万名贫困家庭劳动力进行技术技能培训；面向全省农村贫困县实施定向招生专项计划，使5.07万名学生有更多机会进入名校接受优质高等教育。

grader and her elder sister Li Xiaoyan was attending the high school. As a Chinese saying goes, "Children from poor families tend to be more independent and better prepared to deal with problems." The younger sister Li Kaixuan contemplated dropping out to find employment to ease the family's financial burden.

Three years later in 2017, Dancheng County took the lead in launching the "village-based education chief" mechanism and a total of 3,171 village-based education chiefs and teachers who were responsible, dedicated and well acquainted with local conditions were sent to work in villages to publicize policies relating to poverty alleviation through education, gain an accurate grasp of education-related problems in villages and check for incidences of dropouts. Owing to these efforts, education-related problems among villagers could be timely resolved and all the poor rural students were provided with targeted assistance in a timely manner.

While working in her capacity as a village-based education chief, Liu Guirong learned about what happened to Li Kaixuan and she advised the teenage girl, "In no case should you drop out, as receiving education is the way out and key to changing the lot of your family. Don't worry about the cost for study and living in the school. Leave it to me to deal with it." The following day, Liu Guirong came and offered the girl 3,000 *yuan* and later persisted in donating 500 *yuan* monthly to cover the girl's living expenses.

With the assistance of Liu Guirong and the implementation of poverty alleviation policies such as education subsidy, subsistence allowance and corporate assistance in poverty alleviation, the tuition fees for the two sisters were exempted and the two sisters were provided with a student grant, subsistence allowance, and other forms of financial aid. Meanwhile, arrangements were made for the two girls' mother, Lu Silan, to work as a school dormitory housekeeper. With all these assistance efforts, the family was finally freed from financial worries and the two girls could continue their studies.

In 2018, Li Kaixuan was admitted into Tsinghua University for her academic excellence and her elder sister Li Xiaoyan was also accepted at another university. Under the education-related poverty alleviation policies, the two sisters received relief fund for students from destitute families in each semester throughout their college years. During her college time in Tsinghua University, Li Kaixuan

第二章 攻坚历程

教育扶贫公益培训班
A public welfare training session under the initiative of poverty alleviation through education

河南省组织53所高校与53个贫困县开展校地结对帮扶，高校累计向贫困县提供战略咨询652次，培训专业技术人员49010人次，培训贫困劳动力19077人次，高校定点销售农产品1965吨，提供电商营销服务777次，有力支持了贫困地区经济发展。

通过近年来对贫困地区教育事业的重点支持，截至2020年底，53个贫困县学前教育毛入园率达到97.24%，超过全省平均水平7.74个百分点，小学、初中净入学率均达到或接近全省平均水平。

received the comprehensive financial aid package, including scholarships, student grants, student loans, work-study subsidies, tuition fee exemption, and student allowances. Meanwhile, the two girls also got generous donations from charitable people from many sectors of the society.

The two grateful sisters were eager to do many things in return, joining the school volunteer groups and actively participating in public welfare activities as tokens of gratitude and repayment.

【Panorama】Ensuring Zero Occurrence of Student Dropout Due to Poverty

The initiative of poverty alleviation through education in Henan, revolving around the guarantee of compulsory education, included a series of measures aiming at curbing the discontinuation of education, giving support to business startups, facilitating employment, and boosting industrial development. The implementation of such measures has enabled children from the impoverished families to accept quality education and has served as the key to breaking the cycle of poverty.

The efforts of poverty alleviation through education in Henan have mainly focused on optimizing financial support policies for children from the impoverished families at the compulsory education stage, improving the teaching conditions and facilities in schools in the impoverished regions, and building a stronger team of rural teachers in the impoverished regions. Such efforts also include aiding the secondary vocational schools from the impoverished counties in their professional expansion, establishment of training bases and information construction, and fully tapping universities' strength to boost the industrial development in the impoverished regions.

Since 2016, a total of 5,224,200 students from the registered impoverished families at the compulsory education stage have been given financial support and the funding involved has reached 3,816 million *yuan*. A total of 22,500 primary, middle schools and kindergartens have been newly built or expanded, and 37,200 designated teachers have been recruited to work in the impoverished regions. Vocational training sessions for targeted poverty alleviation have been vigorously organized, providing technical training to 38,200 people from the impoverished

7. 扶贫助残

【故事】集中托养解困境

整洁美观的小院,宽敞明亮的病房,在河南省驻马店市上蔡县大路李乡"重度残疾人托养中心",一名护工一边娴熟地照顾病人吃药,一边柔声细语地同病人聊天。

这名护工叫黄翠英,今年57岁,是上蔡县大路李乡孟尧村居民。

2014年3月,黄翠英的丈夫聂华堂遭遇车祸,成了植物人,黄翠英既要照顾丈夫又要供儿子上学,一家人陷入困境。

黄翠英当时感觉就像天塌了一样。为了给丈夫看病,她花光了家里所有积蓄。聂华堂吃饭得用针管打着吃,每天忙着照顾丈夫,黄翠英常常连饭都顾不上做,整日以泪洗面,精神恍惚。儿子聂锦涛当时正在北方民族大学就读,看到家庭生活困难,他想辍学出去赚钱养家糊口,黄翠英每次听到儿子这样说,眼泪都忍不住流下来。

2016年,大路李乡托养中心恰好启动,凡符合条件的重度残疾人家庭都可以申请入住。

当地政府在评估了黄翠英的家庭状况后,让她的丈夫住进托养中心,同时她也进入托养中心当了一名护工,照顾丈夫和另外一名重症残疾人,每个月工资2000元。

托养中心温暖了黄翠英的心,也温暖着这一家人。没有了家庭的后顾之忧,黄翠英的脸上露出了久违的笑容,儿子也可以安心上学了。

2018年,黄翠英一家正式脱贫,2019年儿子考入四川师范大学就读研究生。

黄翠英家翻天覆地的变化,得益于残疾人集中托养的好政策。黄翠英只是集中托养的受益者之一,与她有着同样感受的还有上蔡县大路李乡肖里侯村的骆荣焕。

2017年,骆荣焕残疾的儿子入住托养中心后,骆荣焕除了每天可以悉心照顾儿子之外,一年还有两万多元的工资。自己吃住不仅不掏钱,

households. Designated enrollment programs targeting students from the impoverished counties have been launched, putting 50,700 students in a better position to get admitted into prestigious universities for high-quality higher education.

In Henan, 53 universities have paired with 53 impoverished counties for poverty alleviation, providing a total of 652 strategic counseling sessions to the impoverished counties and organizing trainings to 49,010 professional technicians and 19,077 impoverished people. Meanwhile, 1,965 tons of agricultural products have been sold through universities and 777 E-commerce marketing sessions have been organized by universities, substantially boosting the economic development of the impoverished regions.

By the end of 2020, with the key support for education in the impoverished regions rolling out in Henan in recent years, the gross enrollment ratio at preschool stage in the 53 impoverished counties had reached 97.24%, 7.74 percentage points higher than the provincial average. Meanwhile the net enrollment ratio for primary schools and junior high schools was close to or even matched the provincial average.

7. Rendering Assistance to the Disabled and Impoverished

【Case】 Institutional Foster Care Lifting Families out of Dilemmas

In a spacious and bright ward in Daluli Town foster care center for the severely disabled in Shangcai County, Zhumadian of Henan Province, a care worker was skillfully administering medicine to a patient while chatting softly with him.

This care worker was none other than the 57-year-old Huang Cuiying, a farmer from Mengyao Village, Daluli Town of Shangcai County in Henan.

In March, 2014, a car accident turned Nie Huatang, Huang Cuiying's husband, into a human vegetable, leaving Huang Cuiying struggling to care for her husband and earning money to pay for their son's education. The family was in severe financial distress.

Huang Cuiying was on the verge of breakdown. She spent all her family savings on treatment for her husband. Every waking moment she was mainly occupied with caring for Nie Huangtang, who needed to be fed with the help of a

赚取的收入还能供小儿子上学。此外，家里的老屋因年久失修漏雨，政府帮她维修了房屋、添置了家具。这在以前是做梦也想不到的事，骆荣焕一家的生活终于有了盼头。

在托养中心工作的护工基本上都是入住者的母亲、妻子或丈夫，在情感上方便照顾病人。而这种托养模式，不仅让残疾人的生活有了保障，更使他们有尊严地活着。

2017年，中国残疾人联合会主席张海迪来到上蔡县，对贫困家庭重度残疾人集中托养工作进行调研，高度评价上蔡县集中托养工作是"托养一人、解脱一家，脱贫一户、温暖一方"。

2019年，上蔡县"贫困家庭重度残疾人集中托养模式"荣获"全球减贫案例有奖征集活动"优秀减贫案例。10月25日，驻马店集中托养模式通过 CHINA DAILY 走向海外，进入全球视野。

【全景】扶贫助残一个不落

残疾人是一个特殊的群体，需要格外关心、格外关注。上蔡县"贫困家庭重度残疾人集中托养模式"被写入《中共中央国务院打赢脱贫攻坚战三年行动的指导意见》《国家乡村振兴战略规划(2018—2022)》和《中国残疾人联合会章程》。

河南省围绕"全面建成小康社会，残疾人一个也不能少"的目标推进扶贫助残工作。在保障残疾人充分享受"两不愁三保障"普惠性政策的同时，建立困难残疾人生活补贴和重度残疾人护理补贴制度，推动重度残疾人照护服务，实施残疾儿童康复救助，将建档立卡重度残疾人家庭无障碍改造与危房改造同步设计、同步施工、同步验收，解决好残疾人康复、托养、无障碍改造等特殊需求，提升残疾人的获得感、幸福感和安全感。

syringe, leaving her little time to prepare food for herself. Worried and exhausted day after day, the tearful Huang Cuiying was trapped in an impossible situation. Worrying about the family finances, her son Nie Jintao, a college student from North Minzu University, proposed dropping out to work to alleviate the family's financial burden. Every time her son brought up the subject of dropping out, Huang Cuiying could not help breaking into tears.

In 2016, the foster care center in Daluli Town was established, to which families with severely disabled members could apply for admission.

After thoroughly evaluating the situation in Huang Cuiying's family, the local government got her husband admitted into the foster care center and arranged for her to work as a care worker there so she could care for her husband and another severely disabled patient. Huang Cuiying could earn 2,000 *yuan* monthly at her new job.

The foster care center brought hope and happiness to Huang Cuiying's family. Free from financial worry, Huang Cuiying became radiant with smiles every day and her son was able to pursue his studies without distraction.

In 2018, Huang Cuiying was officially lifted out of poverty and later in 2019, her son was admitted into Sichuan Normal University for postgraduate study.

These radical changes in Huang Cuiying's family were owed to the initiative of providing institutional foster care to the disabled. Huang Cuiying was not the only beneficiary from this new initiative. Luo Ronghuan, a farmer from Xiaolihou Village, Daluli Town of Shangcai County, also experienced the benefits of the foster care program.

In 2017, Luo Ronghuan's disabled son was admitted into the foster care center where she could take care of her son and work with an annual income of more than 20,000 *yuan*. With board and lodging provided at the center, Luo could spend the bulk of her income on her younger son's schooling. What is more, the local government renovated her leaking old house and even stocked it with furniture. All these good news came to Luo like a dream, paving the way for this family to live a better life.

The care workers at the foster care center are mostly the mothers, wives or husbands of patients, bringing convenience and warmth to the healthcare there. This type of foster care also brings dignity to the patients as well as guarantee of

领取扶贫轮椅
Getting relief wheelchairs

2016年至2020年，河南省累计为5252名建档立卡贫困家庭0—6岁残疾儿童提供康复救助服务，为15.2万人次建档立卡贫困家庭残疾人提供辅助器具适配服务，完成重度残疾人家庭无障碍改造21.3万户，由政府主导的重度残疾人集中托养机构达到1261个，托养重度残疾人23712人。截至2020年8月底，全省有210多万名残疾人享受"两项补贴"。

8. 易地搬迁扶贫

【故事】搬进新社区 幸福来敲门

洛阳市嵩县德亭镇德福苑搬迁社区，宽敞的道路两旁绿树成荫，电子商务服务店、幼儿园、文化广场、运动广场、家风家训馆、文化书屋、扶贫车间、卫生室、社区党群服务中心等一应俱全。

2020年7月1日，德福苑社区几个居民正在休闲广场的树荫下拉家常，脸上洋溢着幸福的微笑。

high-quality care.

In 2017, the Chairperson for China Disabled Persons' Federation, Zhang Haidi, paid a visit to Shangcai County to investigate and research into the institutional foster care service for the severely disabled from the impoverished families. Speaking highly of the foster care service there, Zhang concluded that providing foster care to one person could ease the burden of a whole family, lift one vulnerable household out of poverty and bring warmth to the entire region.

In 2019, the foster care program for the severely disabled from the impoverished families adopted in Shangcai County was recognized as an excellent case for poverty reduction in "Global Solicitation on Poverty Reduction Practices." On October 25 that year, the institutional foster care program adopted in Zhumadian was introduced by *CHINA DAILY* to the world.

【Panorama】 Leaving No One Behind When Rendering Assistance to the Disabled and Impoverished

People with disabilities are a vulnerable group that deserves more public attention and care. The success of the institutional foster care program for the severely disabled from the impoverished families adopted in Shangcai County was included in some government documents, including *The Three-Year Guideline on Winning the Battle Against Poverty* released by the Central Committee of the Communist Party of China and the State Council, *The National Rural Revitalization Strategic Plan (2018-2022)* and *The Charter of China Disabled Persons' Federation*.

Henan has promoted the assistance to the disabled and impoverished with the objective of leaving no disabled person behind in the drive toward building a moderately prosperous society. Apart from ensuring all the disabled people are covered by the inclusive initiative of "two assurances and three guarantees" (assuring the rural poor population that they have adequate food and clothing and guaranteeing them access to compulsory education, basic medical service and safe housing), the mechanism of living subsidies for the disabled people with financial difficulties and of care subsidies for the severely disabled people has been launched, care service for the severely disabled has been bolstered, and rehabilitation assistance for the disabled children has been carried out. The

在这几个居民当中，有一位叫申双利。她住的是一套125平方米三室两厅的房子，客厅里沙发、茶几、电视一应俱全，两个大红的中国结挂在电视两边很是喜庆，申双利正在辅导孩子们做作业，丈夫正在看电视，一家人的日子过得和和美美。

申双利原来住在德亭镇南台村的一个山沟里，交通不便，生产、生活条件差。孩子们上学需要步行半个小时，想出去打工，可孩子们又没人管；不出去打工，在家靠几亩山坡地仅能顾住温饱，遇到旱涝年景种地还得赔钱。

2016年，申双利被评为建档立卡贫困户，享受易地搬迁的扶贫政策。一家人告别了穷山沟搬到了德福苑社区，丈夫外出务工，孩子们就近入学，申双利也能在扶贫车间打工挣钱。收入多了，脱贫了；生活美了，心情好了，每天晚上吃完饭，申双利一家人总会到文化广场散散步、跳跳舞。

在社区有许多年龄较大的贫困户，务工没技术，出力没体力。为了解决这部分人的收入和生活问题，社区专门设置和联系了一些公益岗位，让他们力所能及地有活干有收入。

今年67岁的史毛遂，一家7口人，原来住佛泉寺村的一个山沟里，老伴儿常年瘫痪在床，一家人守着几亩薄地和一些林坡生活，生活不便，收入极少。

住进德福苑社区后，史毛遂一家有了翻天覆地的变化，孩子有的外出务工，有的就近务工，社区把他安排到卫生院做保洁员，每月不仅有1200元的收入，还不耽误照顾老伴儿。史毛遂特别感激易地搬迁的好政策。工作之余，他主动要求做一名志愿者，义务帮助社区打扫卫生。

德福苑社区开办了扶贫车间，用来加工服装和电子产品，在这里务工的都是在社区居住的贫困户。荆秋萍是德亭镇龙王庙村的，原来居住在深山区，外出务工一年多，家中孩子没人管、老人无人照顾，只得放弃务工回家。山里本来地就少，加上旱坡地靠天收，即便种的是好卖的

renovation of handicap-accessible housing for the severely disabled from the registered impoverished households has been synchronized with the renovation of dilapidated housing in terms of design, construction, and evaluation. Efforts have also been made to meet the special needs from the disabled people for rehabilitation, foster care, and renovation of handicap-accessible housing to promote their sense of gain, well-being and security.

Between 2016 and 2020, a total of 5,252 children below the age of six from the registered impoverished households received rehabilitation assistances and assistive devices for persons with disabilities were provided to 152,000 disabled people from the registered impoverished households. Renovations of handicap-accessible housing were conducted among 213,000 households with severely disabled members and a total of 1,261 foster care institutions for the severely disabled were established under the governmental coordination, providing foster care to 23,712 severely disabled patients. By the end of August, 2020, a total of 2.1 million people with disabilities had been granted two subsidies, the living subsidy and care subsidy.

8. Poverty Alleviation through Relocating Poor Households

【Case】 Relocation Bringing Rays of Happiness

Upon stepping into the Defuyuan resettlement community in Deting Town, Songxian County in Luoyang, visitors will be greeted with broad roads lined with lush trees and a cluster of buildings with community public services, including E-commerce service stations, a kindergarten, a culture square, a sports square, a family legacy exhibition hall, bookstores, poverty alleviation workshops, clinics and a community Party and public service center.

On July 1, 2020, radiant with smiles, villagers in this community are chatting under the shady trees on a square.

Among them is Shen Shuangli, who now lives in a three-bedroom apartment with an area of 125 square meters. In the fully-equipped living room with sofas, a coffee table and TV, two red Chinese knots can be seen hanging beside the TV, lending a festive atmosphere to the house. While Shen Shuangli is tutoring the children with their homework, her husband is watching TV, presenting a harmonious scene of family life.

中药材和林果，销售也很困难。

搬进社区后，荆秋萍就近进了扶贫车间务工。山里人不怕吃苦，她很快就成了车间里的"收入状元"，老公也能安心外出务工了，一家人靠劳动脱了贫。

来自杨村村桑树岭的石小涛在社区开办了个电商服务部，他把德亭镇的黑豆、芝麻等土特产和中药材放到网上销售，每月销售额达到1万多元，不仅自己增加了收入，也给镇上的农产品销售开辟了新渠道。

除此之外，社区还开办有家政、种植、电焊、厨师等各类培训班，让搬迁来的群众拥有一技之长，开辟就业渠道。

【全景】易地扶贫搬迁户开启新生活

易地搬迁是贫困群众得到实惠的民生工程，它是解决一方水土养不好一方人的根本。

2016年至2020年，河南深入推进易地扶贫搬迁安置和后续扶持工作，近26万易地扶贫搬迁贫困群众开启了新生活。河南省易地扶贫搬迁工作先后于2017年、2018年、2019年连续三年获得国务院督查激励。

河南省累计投入资金156亿元，新建安置住房7.7万套，将分散在442个乡镇、4145个村的25.97万深山群众，搬到交通便利、生活便捷集中的安置点，建筑总面积约638万平方米，人均面积达24.57平方米，通过"下山""上楼"，实现了从"好房子"到"好日子"的转换。

同步配套水、电、路、网长度约2800千米，集中安置点的安全饮水到户率、生活用电覆盖率、广播电视信号覆盖率、通信集中覆盖率均达到100%；累计建设科教文卫等各类公共服务设施2157个，有小学生的2.32万户搬迁家庭和有中学生的1.61万户搬迁家庭就学条件得到改善，就医条件普遍提升。

However, in the past Shen Shuangli lived in deep mountains in Nantai Village, Deting Town, struggling with harsh living and farming conditions. It took village children half an hour's walk to get to the school because of inadequate roads. Back then, Shen Shuangli was caught in a bind, because going out to find employment meant leaving her children behind unattended while staying in the village to engage in farming meant making the family scrape by on a few *mu* of barren farmland. In times of droughts or floods, Shen could even lose money in farming.

In 2016, after being registered as living in poverty, Shen Shuangli was included in the government initiative of poverty alleviation through relocation. The whole family moved out of the barren mountains to Defuyuan resettlement community. Living in this new community has provided huge convenience for her children to attend schools nearby, for her husband to go out to find work, and for her to work in the poverty alleviation workshop nearby to earn extra money. The mounting family income soon lifted them out of poverty. They now live a happy life and fully enjoy themselves. Every night after supper, the family can go out to the culture square for dancing or jogging.

In this community there were also some aged, impoverished people who lacked physical ability and professional skills to work. To help these people increase their income and make a living and become self-reliant, the community also created or found public welfare jobs for them.

The 67-year-old Shi Maosui used to live in deep mountains in the village of Fuquansi with 6 other family members. His paralyzed wife was confined to bed all the year round. Living purely on several *mu* of barren farmland and woodland, the family had only a meager income and struggled to survive.

After relocating to the Defuyuan community, Shi Maosui's family has undergone unprecedented changes. Some of his children work nearby and others go out to find jobs. Shi Maosui is hired to work as a sanitation worker in the clinic whereby he can earn 1,200 *yuan* monthly and also take care of his wife. Deeply indebted to the initiative of poverty alleviation through relocation, he offers to work as a volunteer to clean the community for free.

A poverty alleviation workshop specializing in the processing of clothing and electronic products was established so that the impoverished residents in the

第二章 攻坚历程

搬迁前后
Two scenes of the same villager before and after the relocation

neighborhood could have work. One of these residents was Jing Qiuping, a local farmer living in deep mountains from Longwangmiao Village, Deting Town. For over a year Jing Qiuping once went out to work, but she had to quit to take care of the young and the elderly at home. The family did not have a stable and adequate source of income as the few farmlands owned by them could not yield much, especially when times were bad. Even when the family switched to growing fruit trees and medical herbs, they still had difficulties finding buyers.

After moving into the resettlement community, Jing Qiuping worked in the nearby poverty alleviation workshop. Her hard work soon made her the top earner in the workshop. Meanwhile, her husband went out to find employment and the family was soon lifted out of poverty.

Shi Xiaotao, a villager from Yangcun Village, now runs an E-commerce service station selling traditional medical herbs and local specialties online like black beans and sesame seeds, from which the high sales volume could reap 10,000 *yuan* per month. The station has not only increased his income, but also created a new sales channel for the local agricultural products in the town.

The local community has also organized some training sessions on a wide range of practical skills, such as housekeeping, planting, welding and cooking, so as to enable the relocated residents to develop skills and have easier access to job opportunities.

【Panorama】 The Relocated Families Embarking on a New Life

As a government initiative aiming to improve the livelihood of the impoverished, poverty alleviation through relocating the poor households is the key to addressing the dilemma facing residents living in the places where local conditions could not sustain their subsistence.

Between 2016 and 2020, with the further implementation of poverty alleviation through relocating the poor households and the follow-up assistance measures, nearly 260,000 impoverished people benefited from this relocation initiative and embarked on a better life. Henan provincial government was highly praised by the State Council for three years consecutively in 2017, 2018, and 2019 for success and excellence in carrying out poverty alleviation through relocation.

A total of 15.6 billion *yuan* has been invested in Henan to fund the relocation

9. 危房改造

【故事】昔日危房 今成"景观"

河南省鲁山县张良镇有一座青龙山,李敏是山下杨李沟村的村民,也是当地农村危房改造工程的受益者。

原本,李敏家里有四间砖瓦结构的老房子,但年久失修,每到下雨时,就是"外面下大雨屋里下小雨",全家人住着老房都担惊受怕,盖新房就成了李敏的心愿。然而,2018年5月,丈夫重病去世花光了家里的积蓄,盖新房的事更是遥遥无期。

2019年7月,李敏家被村里评定为C级危改户,若她家对危旧房屋进行修缮,可以享受1万元的危房改造补贴款。在驻村工作队的帮助下,李敏修补了漏雨跑风的墙缝、修整了凌乱的院落,屋里屋外重新刷了白墙,家里焕然一新。

在杨李沟村,改变的不仅仅是李敏一家,更大的变化则是村容村貌的改善——因为鲁山县在危房改造工作中,开启了拆旧屋、建停车场、游园、花园、果园、菜园的"一场四园"模式,杨李沟村正是这一模式的"策源地"。

在"危房清零"行动中,驻村工作队带领群众拆除危旧房屋21座,新建停车场、农耕展览馆、花园、果园和孝道园、乡愁园、农耕园120余处,以前的石碾、碾盘、石槽等老物件被做成了景观,吸引了不少来休闲的游客。

辛集乡漫流村在实施"一场四园"改造后,村里的12条断头路打通了,改建游园3处、果园2处、菜园6处,人居环境大为改善,曾经脏乱差的"后进村"成了全省农村危房改造现场会观摩的"样板村"。

而在鲁山县四棵树乡黄沟村,"一场四园"带来的不仅有"面子",还有"里子"。2018年以来,借助"天然氧吧"的自然条件,黄沟村通过危房改造,修缮了一些还能居住的旧房子,吸引城里游客来体验田园生活。其中8户群众的闲置房屋被开发成"自助式农家院",通过入

of the impoverished population, building a total of 77,000 new houses in the resettlement area and moving 259,700 impoverished people who used to live in deep mountains from 4,145 villages of 442 towns to resettlement sites which feature easy access to transportation and convenience in the daily life. The overall construction area of involved in the relocation has reached 6.38 million square meters, with the area of per person amounting to 24.57 square meters. Through "moving down the hill" and "getting upstairs," the otherwise impoverished population now can find access to better housing and a chance for a better life.

Additionally, more than 2,800 kilometers of paved roads have been built with access to water, electricity and broadband Internet simultaneously put in place. Each household's access to safe drinking water, electricity, radio and TV signal, and telecommunication signal has been one hundred percent guaranteed in the resettlement area. A total of 2,157 public service facilities have been established for scientific, educational, cultural, and medical purposes. A total of 23,200 relocated households with primary school students and 16,100 households with middle school students can access better schools for their children and enjoy better medical care.

9. Renovation of Dilapidated Housing

【Case】 The Once Dilapidated Houses Now Transfigured into Delightful Landscape

At the foot of the Qinglong Mountain in Zhangliang Town, Lushan County of Henan, the village of Yangligou can be found. Li Min is a local villager and beneficiary of the initiative of renovating dilapidated housing.

In the past, Li Min lived in a four-room house built of bricks and tiles. Due to inadequate maintenance over the years, rainy days would see the house leaking everywhere, a constant headache and worry for the family. Renovating the house became Li Min's burning aspiration, but she was mercilessly frustrated and the renovation of the house was indefinitely delayed when in May 2018 all the family savings were spent on medical treatment for her husband after he was struck by a severe disease and died.

In July, 2019, Li Min's family was rated by the local government as a C-level household eligible for housing renovation, whereby she was entitled to

股分红、带动就业等方式,帮助群众增收。

因农村危房改造工作有成效、有创新,2020年5月8日,国务院办公厅印发通报,对2019年落实有关重大政策措施成效明显的地方予以督查激励,鲁山县被评为2019年河南省农村危房改造工作积极主动、成效明显的县。

【全景】下足"绣花"功夫改造农村危房

习近平总书记多次强调"让贫困人口不住危房"。河南省住房城乡建设系统下足"绣花"功夫,认真细致推进农村危房改造工作,让贫困群众住上了安全的房屋。

在工作中,先由住房建设、扶贫等多部门协同办公,精准确定住房改造对象,然后组织专业鉴定机构对危房进行鉴定,再根据具体情况采取不同的改造方案。其中,针对部分鳏寡孤独、无力筹措资金的特困户,通过多种措施解决其住房问题,如统一建设农村集体公租房、幸福大院,置换、租赁闲置农房,修缮加固闲置公房等。这样一来,不仅节约了土地,又方便农户之间相互照料、互助养老。

住上新房
Getting relocated into the new house

a renovation allowance of 10,000 *yuan* to put into her dilapidated house. With the help from the village-based work team, Li Min had the leaking ceilings and walls repaired and whitewashed. Meanwhile, improvements were also made to the disorderly courtyard. After renovations, the interior and exterior of her house took on a new look.

In Yangligou Village, changes went far beyond the renovation of individual houses like Li Min's. More spectacular changes could be seen in the improvement of natural and living conditions in the village. As part of the renovation efforts for dilapidated housing in Lushan County, efforts also went into the construction of "one lot and four gardens," namely the parking lot, leisure garden, flower garden, orchard, and vegetable garden, resulting from the extensive renovation efforts initiated in Yangligou Village.

When the campaign of "reducing dilapidated housing to zero" went into full swing in the village, the work teams helped with the demolition of 21 dilapidated houses and the building of 120-plus public service facilities, including a parking lot, an exhibition hall for agricultural activities, gardens, orchards, a filial piety theme park, a nostalgia theme park and a farm garden. Traditionally used instruments like stone rollers (for threshing grain), millstones and stone troughs were put on display, attracting many urban visitors on leisure tours.

The implementation of "one lot and four gardens" renovation project in Manliu Village of Xinji Town led to 12 dead-end roads being extended and 3 gardens, 2 orchards and 6 vegetable gardens newly built or rebuilt. The village has undergone amazing improvements in living conditions. It is a miracle that this once dirty, disorderly, and dilapidated village has become an exemplary demonstration village for an on-the-spot provincial meeting on renovation of rural dilapidated housing in Henan.

In Huanggou Village, Sikeshu Town of Lushan County, the "one lot and four gardens" renovation project has given the village a facelift and provided greater income for villagers. Since 2018, making the most of the forest resources to serve as natural oxygen bars, the village has renovated some inhabitable old houses to attract urban visitors who are fascinated with rural experience. Under this initiative, 8 idle houses from villagers have been transformed into self-help farmyards, greatly boosting villagers' income through creating more jobs and

脱贫攻坚战以来，河南省累计为57.8万户贫困群众完成了危房改造，这些群众主要包括建档立卡贫困户、低保户、农村分散供养特困人员和贫困残疾人家庭。

2018年和2019年，河南省连续两年被住建部、财政部确定为农村危房改造工作积极主动、成效明显的省份，受到国务院的表彰。2020年上半年，河南省完成了"全省存量危房全部清零"的目标任务。

10. 扶贫扶志

【故事】乡村"秀才"脱贫记

王万才是河南省唐河县城郊乡农民，1964年12月出生。虽然只有初中文化，但他不仅练就一手好字，对联、诗词、文章也写得不错，很早就用手机注册了微博、微信，和网友进行创作交流，被村民们亲切地称为"王秀才"。

王万才妻子患病，儿子先天智障，他用辛勤种地、抽空务工攒下的钱领着儿子四处求治，但仍毫无起色。2014年春，王万才到工地上去干活，结果不慎摔伤，做完手术后身负重债。要强的他觉得这辈子彻底失败了，终日借酒浇愁，成了村里有名的"酒星子"。

2016年1月17日，村里老支书告诉王万才，他被精准识别为贫困户，政府要帮他脱贫了。而此时，他对脱贫的愿望并不强烈，因为之前也努力过，数次失败已让他失去了信心。针对王万才意志消沉的情况，县、乡扶贫干部鼓励他："你是咱县想脱贫、会脱贫的代表，你一定要给贫困群众干出个样儿来！"一语破心结，这些鼓励让王万才精神头儿抖起来了。

在驻村干部和工作队的帮助下，2016年，王万才尝试转租土地种地膜西瓜，当年就卖了1.8万元。除了地里的收成，县乡村根据政策给王万才全家办了低保、地力补贴、电费补贴、农业保险、人身意外伤害保险，妻子有了慢性病诊疗卡、儿子有了残疾人补贴，这些惠民政策的

paying out dividends from entity investment.

On May 8, 2020, the General Office of the State Council issued an announcement to acclaim regions achieving genuine results in implementing key national policies, in which Lushan County was highly acclaimed and listed as the county making prominent achievements in the renovation of rural dilapidated housing on account of its success and innovation in this regard.

【Panorama】Meticulously Engaging in Renovation of Rural Dilapidated Housing

Chinese President Xi Jinping spoke about the urgency for "no impoverished population living in dilapidated housing" on many occasions. Echoing his concern, the bureaus of Henan Provincial Housing and Urban-Rural Development at different levels carried out the renovation of rural dilapidated housing prudently and meticulously, providing all impoverished people with safe housing.

The coordination of multiple departments responsible for housing and urban-rural development and poverty alleviation has concentrated efforts into first accurately identifying the targets for housing renovation, then organizing the specialized rating agencies to rate the dilapidated housing and finally formulating and implementing the renovation plans tailored to the specific conditions. For those deeply impoverished households who had no kith and kin and could not raise the money for renovation, a series of measures have been adopted to address their problems, including constructing government-funded rural collective rental housing and a multi-service center for the elderly, encouraging the exchange and renting of idle rural houses and renovating idle collectively-owned village houses. The implementation of these measures has saved the precious land resources and also brought convenience for mutual care and assistance in the care of the elderly.

The initiative of renovating dilapidated housing has benefited a total of 578,000 impoverished households in Henan since the launch of the fight against poverty. The initiative mainly focuses on four priority groups: households registered as living in poverty, households eligible for subsistence allowances, individuals living in extreme poverty or basic assistance in rural areas and families of people with disabilities affected by poverty.

Listed by the Ministry of Housing and Urban-Rural Development and

滋润，让王万才觉得日子有了奔头。

2017年春，看到花生行情好，王万才采用新技术种了10亩地膜花生，政府派农艺师免费做技术培训，他又大获丰收。2017年末，王万才家人均纯收入达到5800元，顺利实现了脱贫。

到了春节，王万才写了两副春联贴在自家门口，一副是"秋水半瓢邀月饮，春风十里荷锄归"，另一副是"和谐普世东风化雨，精准扶贫老树逢春"，写下了对美好生活的无限向往。他的网名，从"老树西风"改成了"老树逢春"。

2018年春天，王万才被选为唐河县劳动模范。精神振奋的他又在自家小院里干起了豆腐坊，家庭收入再次提高。作为"文化人"的王万才，出版了《唐河千帆过——王万才脱贫日记选》一书，被评为"中原传媒好书"。

人勤地不懒
The land yielding well with an industrious planter

the Ministry of Finance as the province making prominent achievements in the renovation of rural dilapidated housing in 2018 and 2019, Henan Province was commended by the State Council for the efforts in this regard. In the first half of 2020, Henan successfully reached the goal of reducing the existing dilapidated housing to zero across the province.

10. Poverty Reduction through Stimulating Internal Momentum
【Case】 The Village Scholar Eliminating Poverty

Wang Wancai was born in December 1964 to a rural family in Tanghe County, Henan Province. Although he only had junior middle school education, his handwriting was graceful and he was skilled in writing couplets, poems, and essays. He registered accounts at Microblog and WeChat with his cellphone to communicate with other web writers, leading villagers to affectionately call him "Scholar Wang."

Wang Wancai's wife was sick, and his son suffered from congenital mental retardation, forcing him to till hard in the fields and accept many part-time jobs. With the money earned he sought medical treatment for his son, but no miracle came. In the spring of 2014, Wang Wancai took a part-time job at a construction site to make money, but unfortunately fell and was badly injured. A necessary operation crushed him under a load of heavy debts. Though a tough guy, he became frustrated and saw no hope left in his life. Wang tried to drown his sorrows in wine every day and soon became the village drunkard.

On January 17, 2016, the old Party secretary in the village gave Wang Wancai great news that his family had been accurately identified as a poverty-alleviation household and the government was about to help him eliminate poverty. Wang Wancai was not thrilled about the news at first because he had tried so many times and failed, consuming all his patience and confidence. Considering Wang's lack of motivation, the county and town poverty alleviation officials encouraged him, "In our county, among those who need to get out of poverty, you are the one who has the greatest ability to make it. And thus you're responsible for setting an example for them all!" The words pulled on his heartstrings and revitalized him.

With the help of village-baed officials and work team, Wang tried subleasing land to grow watermelons with plastic mulch in 2016. The attempt was successful

脱贫后的王万才于2019年加入了中国共产党，热心参与村里大大小小的事务。2020年疫情防控期间，他申请到村口执勤，回村又主动当起了政策宣传员。2020年底，王万才获得"2020年全国脱贫攻坚奖奋进奖"。

2021年，唐河县城郊乡正在打造"生态田园小镇"，王万才也要参与其中，发展新的产业。

【全景】既"富脑袋"又"富口袋"

2019年9月，习近平总书记在光山县考察时再次叮嘱，扶贫要和扶智扶志相结合，让贫困群众脱贫后的生活芝麻开花节节高。

脱贫攻坚战打响以来，河南针对部分贫困群众动力不足、精神懈怠的突出问题，不再采用送钱送物的扶贫方式，而是根据既"富脑袋"又"富口袋"的思路，深入做好群众的思想工作，将他们对美好生活的渴望转变为脱贫的动力。

加强教育引导和政策引导。河南省广泛进行脱贫政策、脱贫故事、脱贫经验的宣讲和扶贫政策宣传解读，让群众充分了解政策；出台专项政策鼓励贫困群众参与到脱贫攻坚中。同时，采取以工代赈、生产奖补、劳务补助等方式对率先脱贫群众进行激励，倡导多劳多得、勤劳致富。

做好文化扶贫。河南省加快基层综合性文化服务中心、公共图书馆、文化馆等文化基础设施建设，利用农民夜校、"中原文化大舞台"、"戏曲进农村"等平台和活动，强化对贫困地区的文化服务，引导贫困群众摒弃消极思想、增强自主脱贫信心。

and yielded 18,000 *yuan* that year. In line with policies the county and village governments also ensured that his family could enjoy basic living allowance, soil fertility subsidies, electricity subsidies, and covered agricultural insurance and personal accident insurance for the family. His wife received a chronic disease diagnosis and treatment card and his son received a disability subsidy. These benefits joined to nourish Wang Wancai and he began feeling hopeful for his life.

In the spring of 2017, when the peanut market was good, Wang Wancai used a new technology to plant 10 *mu* of peanuts with plastic mulch. The government sent agronomists to offer free technical training and helped him reap another bumper harvest. By the end of 2017, Wang's per capita net income had reached 5,800 *yuan*, successfully lifting him out of poverty.

That year during the Spring Festival, the traditional Chinese New Year, Wang Wancai wrote two pairs of Spring Festival couplets and posted them beside his doors. One pair read, "With half a ladle of water I happily invited the moon to drink with me, intoxicated in ten miles of breeze I came home with my hoe on the shoulder." The other couplet read, "The east wind brings rain for the crops in the harmonious society, and targeted poverty alleviation revitalizes this old tree." These couplets expressed Wang's new infinite hope for a better life. Wang Wancai even changed his Internet name from "A Veteran Tree in the West Wind" to "A Veteran Tree Revitalized in Spring."

In the spring of 2018, Wang Wancai was selected as a labor model in Tanghe County. Bucked up by the achievement, Wang opened a bean curd mill in his yard, which brought him much more profit. As a "cultured man," Wang Wancai published a book entitled *A Thousand Sails Passing by in Tanghe County—Wang Wancai's Selected Journals on Poverty Alleviation*, which has been rated as "Central Plains Media Good Book."

Newly free from poverty, Wang joined the Communist Party of China (CPC) in 2019 and enthusiastically participated in the village's public affairs. During the epidemic prevention and control period in 2020, he asked to perform guard duty at the village entrance and took the initiative to work as a policy publicist when he got back. At the end of 2020, Wang Wancai won the 2020 National Poverty Alleviation Award.

In 2021, the suburban village of Tanghe County is creating "an ecological

农民夜校
A night school for the farmers in the new era

发挥典型引导作用。河南省注重从群众身边发掘、树立脱贫先进典型，发挥榜样的示范带动效应，引导更多贫困群众向先进学习、力争早日脱贫。

2016 年至 2019 年，河南贫困地区农村居民年人均可支配收入年均增长 10.8%，比全省农村平均水平高 1.8 个百分点。

11. 交通扶贫

【故事】前何村的"泥水路"变成了水泥路

韩宇南是周口市税务局的一名普通干部，2015 年 8 月，受一部扶贫题材的电视剧《马向阳下乡记》的影响，他主动申请到太康县马厂镇前何村担任第一书记，驻村扶贫。

韩宇南第一次入村的时候，正赶上一场大雨过后，村路泥泞不堪，成群的鹅在路上的水坑里游着，他是"溜着墙根"进村上任的。

pastoral town." Wang Wancai is also interested and plans to develop new industries there.

【Panorama】 Enriched both Spiritually and Materially

When visiting Guangshan County in September 2019, General Secretary Xi Jinping once again urged that enlightenment and initiative mobilization should synchronize with poverty alleviation so that the poor people's living standards would rise like sesame flowering successively high.

Confronted with poor people's lack of internal momentum, Henan government abandoned the method of providing money and goods for the poor at the start of the battle against poverty. They instead adopted the strategy of enriching people both spiritually and materially, and managed to encourage people to brave it out and to turn their desire for a better life into internal momentum to drive the fight against poverty.

One such method is to reinforce exhortation and policy guidance. Henan Province has extensively publicized and interpreted poverty alleviation policies, stories, and experiences to make sure that the public can fully understand them. Policies tailored to individual villages are also introduced to encourage poor people to participate in the fight against poverty. At the same time, the first people to be lifted out of poverty will be encouraged by means of work relief, production awards and labor subsidies. These policies advocate gaining more by working harder and growing wealthy through industriousness.

Another method for alleviating poverty is through culture infusion. Henan Province has accelerated the construction of cultural infrastructure such as community-level comprehensive cultural service centers, public libraries, and cultural centers, and has made use of platforms and activities such as farmers' night schools, the Grand Stage of Central Plains Culture and Opera to the Countryside, so as to enhance cultural services for the impoverished areas to help poor people abandon negative thoughts and to boost their confidence in poverty alleviation.

A third method of poverty alleviation is to give play to the role of models. Henan Province has attached great importance to discovering and setting up advanced models of poverty alleviation from the masses, so that they then

前何村的贫困模样深深刺痛了来自农村家庭的韩宇南。当时前何村共有595户2322人,其中贫困户有175户784人。"宁摸十里黑,不走何庄街",说的就是前何村,外村的姑娘都不愿嫁到这里来。

要想富,先修路。韩宇南在驻村的第一个夜晚失眠了,他决定要干的第一件事就是修路。

韩宇南想方设法争取到800万元的道路扶贫专项资金,但修路需要先垫路基,土从哪里取,人手哪里找,具体困难一大堆。

时值严冬,韩宇南与村干部一起顶着寒风,走遍驻村所辖的5个自然村,逐村逐街进行实地丈量。他白天测量街道,晚上回到住处后,将测量的数据绘制成图,申报规划。4个多月时间,为修整路基全村共出动1100多人次劳力,就凭一台挖掘机、10辆四轮车,挖坑塘取土800多车,垫平了村里坑坑洼洼的路。终于,连接5个自然村的11公里"泥水路"变成了实实在在的水泥路。临近春节,两位瘫痪在家十多年的老人,也被家人用轮椅推到大街上,见见乡里乡亲,晒晒冬日暖阳,别提多高兴了。

交通便利了,农产品"走出去"成为可能,韩宇南积极引导村民种植辣椒、大蒜、西瓜等经济型作物,收入有了大幅提高。随后,他又因户制宜,对贫困户开展技能培训,帮助他们外出务工;调整种植结构,引导村民以"公司+农户"的方式发展经济作物产业;对有技术的能手,协助贷款发展规模养殖业。2018年,前何村顺利退出贫困村序列。

如今的前何村,路宽了、灯亮了、树绿了,打了机井、修了桥梁,农民体育广场、党群服务中心建好了,扶贫车间开工了,光伏电站发电了,小学教学楼建起来了,天然气入村了,自来水、电力、宽带户户通,老百姓的脸上挂满了笑容。

驻村第一书记两年一个任期,因村民联名挽留,2015年起韩宇南在前何村一干就是4年。两期结束,为了巩固脱贫成果,他再次决定留下。"前何不富,不回税务。"践行着当初的承诺,怀揣着对村民的感情,韩宇南脚步不停,带领前何村踏上了更广阔的致富路。

function as role models for others to look up to and spur others to shake off poverty as soon as possible.

From 2016 to 2019, the annual per capita disposable income of rural residents in the impoverished areas in Henan increased by 10.8%, 1.8 percentage points higher than the provincial average level in rural areas.

11. Poverty Alleviation through Transportation Improvement

【Case】 Mud Roads Turned to Cement Roads in Qianhe Village

Han Yunan used to be an ordinary official in Zhoukou Tax Bureau. In August 2015 he watched a poverty-alleviation TV series titled *Ma Xiangyang's Journey to the Rural Area* and was moved. He volunteered to be the village-based first secretary in Qianhe Village, Machang Town, Taikang County, resolved to help free them from poverty.

It was after a heavy rain that Han Yunan first entered the village. He was impressed by how muddy the roads were in the village. Rain puddles here and there hosted flocks of geese swimming happily. To find some drier place to put his feet, Han had to tread along the wall foot into the village, not unlike a thief sneaking against the wall.

The poverty in Qianhe Village made Han Yunan, a man who grew up in a rural family, astonished and unsettled. The village at that time had a total of 595 households with 2,322 people, among which 175 households with 784 people were stricken by poverty. There was a local saying about Qianhe Village, "Rather travel ten more miles in the dark than tread on the roads in Qianhe Village." For that reason, no girl from neighboring villages would like to marry into the village.

If you want to be rich, build the road first. Han Yunan lost sleep on his first night in the village when he determined that the first thing he should do was to build the roads.

Han Yunan tried every means to obtain 8 million *yuan* special funds for road building in poor areas, but money was not the only problem. To build a road, the roadbed must first be laid. Then came a bundle of practical problems such as where to collect earth and where to find the hands to do the work.

Han Yunan and village officials walked against the cold wind in severe winter through the five natural villages under the jurisdiction of Qianhe Administrative

【全景】打通百姓"特色致富路"

贫困地区多集中在交通不便的深山地区,"出门硬化路、雨天不踩泥、抬脚上客车、物流到家门"是群众最迫切的愿望。

河南以交通扶贫新模式打通百姓"特色致富路",基本形成了以县城为中心、乡镇为节点、建制村为网点的"外通内联、通村畅乡"的农村公路网络、"辐射周边、循环互补"的城乡客运网络。

完成建制村"两通"兜底任务是交通扶贫的基础指标,至2019年6月,河南省建制村通硬化路率达到100%,具备条件的建制村通客车率达到100%,所有易地搬迁安置区均实现至少有一条通畅的对外出口路。

山崖上凿岩修路
Drilling rocks on the cliff to open a road

河南省实施农村公路"百县通村入组工程"和乡村客运"万村通客车提质工程"。2019年以来,全省累计新增2.7万个20户以上的自然

Village and measured the roads one after another. He did the measurement in the daytime and integrated the data into a table back at his residence at night for his report. In over 4 months, with merely an excavator and 10 four-wheelers, more than 1,100 people from the village dug out more than 800 loads of earth and raised all the roadbeds. Finally, the 11-kilometer mud roads connecting the five natural villages became cement roads. As the Spring Festival approached, two paralyzed seniors who had stayed at home for more than 10 years were wheeled out to the streets by their families to meet the villagers and to bask in the warm winter sun. Their joy was beyond imagination.

With convenient transportation, it was possible for agricultural products to go to market. Han Yunan actively guided villagers to plant economic crops such as pepper, garlic, and watermelon, which greatly increased their income. Later, he provided training for poor households to help them develop skills to work as migrant labors. He adjusted the planting structure and guided the villagers to cooperate with companies to develop cash crop industries. For skilled hands, he helped them secure bank loans to develop large-scale breeding industries. As a result, Qianhe Village successfully exited from the poor villages list in 2018.

Now in Qianhe Village, the roads are wide, the lights are bright, the trees are green, the machine well is drilled, the bridge is rebuilt, and the peasant sports square is constructed. They also have the Party branch and the masses service center and have started the poverty alleviation workshop. The photovoltaic power station has successfully started working and the primary school building is ready to welcome kids. Natural gas is channeled into the village, and every household can enjoy running water, power and broadband now. Smiles are always on the face of every villager.

When his two-year tenure as first secretary of the village came to the end, all the villagers begged Han Yunan to stay in a joint petition. Han agreed and worked for 4 years in Qianhe Village since 2015. When the second term came to the end, he once again decided to stay in the village in order to consolidate their achievements in poverty alleviation. "I won't go back to Zhoukou Tax Bureau until Qianhe Village finally becomes rich." declared Han. With affection for the villagers, Han Yunan never stops to fulfill his original commitment to them and keeps leading Qianhe Village onto a broader road to prosperity.

村通硬化路，新增、调整贫困地区农村客运班线 964 条，新增农村客运车辆 1691 辆。

太行山上的盘山公路
The winding mountain road on the Taihang Mountain

2016 至 2020 年，河南省实施"交通+旅游""交通+搬迁""交通+产业"等交通扶贫新模式，全省贫困地区新改建农村公路 38831 千米，为全省贫困地区打造资源路、旅游路、产业路等"特色致富路"总里程 2564 千米，创建国家级"四好农村路示范县"10 个，数量居全国第一。

【Panorama】 Opening Up the Featured Road to Prosperity for People

Poverty-stricken areas are mostly concentrated in remote mountain areas where traffic is inconvenient. What people there want most badly is seeing hardened roads when going out, not having to drag their feet in the mud when it rains, having buses to board and logistics to their doors.

With the new model of poverty alleviation through transportation, Henan has opened up a road to prosperity for people. A rural road network has been built with the county as the center, the towns as nodes and administrative villages as lattice points. The network connects the inside with the outside, villages with towns, and serves as an urban and rural passenger transport network, radiating the surrounding places and providing circulation and complementary travel.

It is the basic objective of poverty alleviation through transportation to fulfill the preliminary task of "the two openings" to help the poor in administrative villages. By June 2019, 100% of the administrative villages in Henan Province had had hardened roads, 100% of qualified villages had had access to buses, and all relocation areas had had at least one unobstructed road out.

Henan Province implemented the "Extending Hardened Roads to Natural Villages and Rural Groups in 100 Counties" and "Extending Bus Access to Numerous Villages and Elevating the Service Quality" projects. Since 2019, hardened roads have been extended to a total of 27,000 newly increased villages with more than 20 households, 964 rural passenger lines in the poverty-stricken areas have been opened or adjusted, and 1,691 new passenger vehicles have been installed in rural areas in Henan.

Between 2016 and 2020, Henan implemented new models of poverty alleviation through transportation improvement, including "transportation plus tourism," "transportation plus relocation," and "transportation plus industries." 38,831 kilometers of rural roads were rebuilt in the poverty-stricken areas of the province, and 2,564 kilometers of characteristic roads to prosperity were created, such as resources roads, tourism roads, industry roads and others. Ten state-level Model Counties with Four-Good Rural Roads were established, with the number ranking first in China.

12. 水利扶贫

【故事】甘甜的井水流入千万家

毛张村是平顶山叶县仙台镇一个不起眼的村庄，2018年之前，全村246户村民吃水全靠自家打的浅井，但浅井水质不好，每次烧开水，水壶里总是留下厚厚的一层水垢。毛张村的村民们无一不期盼早日吃上深井水。

2018年，叶县农村饮水安全工程覆盖该村。6月初，毛张村饮水安全工程正式开始施工。施工队不顾天气炎热，每天加班加点赶进度，十几台挖掘机交叉作业。有时遇上下大雨，雨水灌进刚开挖好的埋管沟，天一放晴施工队就赶快清淤，一刻也不耽误。工程进度快时，一天能铺设管道1000多米。当通水管道铺到群众家门口时，村民们常常送西瓜给施工队表达心意。

经过施工队一个多月的努力，7月20日正式通水。这个工程包括两口130米的深井，储水罐日供水能力50吨，管道长度7000余米，能够满足辖区6个自然村的用水需求。

叶县常村镇毛洞村的饮水安全工程也是这个时期完成的。和仙台镇平坦的地势相比，多山的常村镇施工难度更大。

2018年6月底开始施工时，井打到20多米深的时候打不动了，因为乱石太多，打20多米就要耗时一个月。这时候，施工队不得不更换更大型号的钻井机，而每更换一次，就要用三台载重20多吨的大货车把之前的机械撤走。为打这口井，钻井机从-60型号、-80型号一直换到了最大的-600型号。经过约两个月的建设，工程完工。该工程的储水罐就在村南边的空旷地带上，检测人员从罐旁边的自流井里取样检测，确认水质达到饮用水的标准，毛洞村村民终于喝上了清凉甘甜的井水。

在叶县的其他乡镇施工中，也常遇到各种复杂的问题，如常村镇艾小庄村的井甚至打到400米深才出水；夏李乡苗庄村打了3口井都没有水，直到第4口井才成功……这些困难都没能阻挡农村饮水安全工程的

12. Poverty Reduction through Water Conservancy Efforts

【Case】 Sweet Phreatic Water into Thousands of Households

Maozhang Village is an obscure village in Xiantai Town, Ye County in Pingdingshan area. Before 2018, all 246 households in the village relied on their own self-drilled wells for drinking water. The water from shallow wells was poor in quality and a thick layer of limescale came up in the kettle every time the water was boiled. The villagers of Maozhang Village looked forward to having a deep well soon for drinking water.

The rural drinking water safety project in Ye County got officially started in Maozhang Village in early June, 2018. Despite hot weather, the construction team worked overtime every day to speed the project with more than a dozen excavators constantly working. Sometimes in the case of heavy rain, when the just-finished trench for tubes were filled with rainwater, the construction team would remove silt as soon as the weather cleared up without a moment's delay. When the construction progressed well, more than 1,000 meters of pipeline could be laid in one day. When the drinking water pipeline approached people's dwellings, the villagers usually brought watermelons to the construction team to express their thanks.

After more than a month of effort, the project officially came online on July 20. This project includes two 130-meter-deep wells with 50 tons of daily supply capacity from a water storage tank and a pipeline of over 7,000 meters long, which can successfully meet the needs of 6 natural villages in Maozhang Village.

The rural drinking water safety project of Maodong Village, Changcun Town, Ye County was also completed during this period. Compared with the flat terrain in Xiantai Town, the construction was much more difficult in the mountainous Changcun Town.

The construction began at the end of June 2018, but work could not go on when the drill went down about 20 meters. There were so many rocks that it cost a month to drill about 20 meters. The team had to replace the drill with a larger one, and each time it took three trucks with 20 tons of load capacity to get the previous drill removed. To dig this well, drills were changed from model-60 to model-80, then all the way to the largest model-600. After about two months of

步伐。

2018年，叶县把农村饮水安全工程列入该县"十大重点民生工程"，筹资2亿多元对全县存在饮水隐患和饮水困难的295个行政村全部实施了自来水工程。至2018年10月底，所有工程全部完工，全县农村安全饮水实现全覆盖，554个行政村、70多万群众全部吃上了安全放心的自来水，彻底告别了"吃水难"。

【全景】确保群众吃上安全水、放心水

"十三五"期间，根据实际情况，河南省构建了合理的水利脱贫攻坚制度体系，涵盖贫困人口饮水安全、水利基础设施升级、水库移民增收、城乡一体化供水试点等方面，并将重点放到贫困人口饮水安全上。水利部门明确每个年度的目标，并将责任进行分包，完善管理制度，如期完成全省农村饮水安全脱贫攻坚"双百"达标，即到2020年实现贫困人口饮水安全百分之百达标、农村饮水安全工程从"源头"到"龙头"的百分之百过程管理。

"十三五"以来，全省水利系统共落实农村饮水安全巩固提升工程建设资金94.08亿元，受益人口2418万人；贫困地区水利基础设施大为改善；全省水库移民人均收入稳步增长；平顶山、濮阳两市"城乡供水一体化"试点初见成效，为全省水利工作提供了经验。

至2020年6月底，全省共建成农村集中供水工程21119处，7600万人享受到集中供水带来的便利，吃上了放心水。全国"十三五"规划中，农村集中供水率的目标是85%，而河南省集中供水率达93%、自来水普及率达91%，超额完成了目标。

construction, the project was completed. A water storage tank was installed in the open area south of the village. The inspectors took samples from the artesian well next to the tank and confirmed that the water quality met the requirements for drinking water. The villagers in Maocong Village finally could enjoy refreshing and sweet drinking water from the well.

The construction in other towns in Ye County were also confronted with various complicated problems. For example, the well in Aixiaozhuang Village of Changcun Town did not yield water until the drill had gone down 400 meters deep. In Miaozhuang Village of Xiali Town, the first three wells failed to work. They did not give up, and the fourth well finally rewarded them with water. However, none of these difficulties had ever stopped the progressing of rural drinking water safety project.

In 2018, Ye County listed the rural drinking water safety project as one of the county's ten key livelihood projects, raising more than 200 million *yuan* to implement water supply engineering in 295 administrative villages with drinking water risks and difficulties. By the end of October 2018, all the projects had been completed, and safe drinking water was available to all rural residents in the county. More than 700,000 people in 554 administrative villages had access to safe tap water, putting an end to drinking water difficulties.

【Panorama】 Seeing to It that People Have Access to Safe Water

During the 13th Five-Year Plan period, Henan Province has established a reasonable water conservancy poverty alleviation system, ensuring safety of drinking water for the poor, upgrading water conservancy infrastructure, increasing income of the relocation people for reservoirs construction, experimenting with an integrated urban and rural water supply pilot project, but the focus was always the safety of drinking water for the poor. The water conservancy department has defined the annual goals, subcontracted the responsibilities, improved the management system, and completed on schedule the province's "two 100%" goal in terms of poverty alleviation through ensuring rural drinking water safety, that is, 100% standardization of rural drinking water and 100% process management of the rural drinking water from source to taps by 2020.

Since the implementation of the 13th Five-Year Plan, the provincial water

新县水源区封育治理
Closing the mountain to cultivate the forest and sealing the slope to cultivate grass in Xinxian County water source area

13. 电网升级和网络扶贫

【故事】"麦小登"的新田园故事

王晓楠是河南省安阳市滑县一个"95后"农家妹，她给自己起了个网名叫"麦小登"，寓意"五谷丰登"。近两年，"麦小登"用短视频记录农家生活，吸引了众多粉丝。

几间红砖平房，垂满枝头的李子、葡萄，一方菜圃、三两鸡雏，"麦小登"家的小院简朴却充满生机。这里，是"麦小登"视频创作的主要场所。

conservancy system has put a total of 9.408 billion *yuan* into the project to maintain and improve rural drinking water safety, benefiting 24.18 million people. As a result, water conservancy infrastructure in poor areas has been greatly improved and the per capita income of the relocated people because of reservoir construction has increased steadily. The pilot project of integrated urban and rural water supply in Pingdingshan City and Puyang City has achieved initial success, providing guidance for water conservancy work for the whole province.

By the end of June 2020, Henan Province had completed a total of 21,119 rural centralized water supply projects, providing 76 million people with the convenience of centralized water supply and safe water. The 13th Five-Year Plan prescribed that the centralized water supply rate in rural areas should reach 85%. Henan's centralized water supply rate has reached 93% and tap water popularization rate has reached 91%, exceeding the objective.

13. Power Grid Upgrade and Poverty Alleviation through Internet

【Case】Mai Xiaodeng's Stories of a New Countryside

Wang Xiaonan is a young peasant girl born after 1995 in Hua County, Anyang City, Henan Province. She uses Mai Xiaodeng, or "Good Harvests," as her online name. For two years, Mai Xiaodeng has attracted many fans with short videos showing her rural life.

With a few red brick bungalows, plums and grapes hanging on the branches, a vegetable garden with a couple of chicks, the small courtyard of Mai Xiaodeng's family is simple but full of vitality. This is where Mai Xiaodeng makes most of her videos.

The Mai Xiaodeng we see through camera lens wears braids and loves to talk and laugh, but few people know that in real life she once was poverty-stricken, that she once felt self-abased for her poor family, and that she was once a lost wanderer.

Mai Xiaodeng grew up in a single-parent family and had to rely on neighbors for food and other necessities. In 2013, Mai Xiaodeng's family was identified as a poverty-stricken household. With 2,000 *yuan* scraped together by relatives, she was able to realize her dream of attending college. After graduation, Mai Xiaodeng successively worked as an editor, a seller at a stall, a part-time teacher,

镜头里的"麦小登",扎着麻花辫,爱说、爱笑,可很少人知道,镜头之外的她曾是一名贫困户,曾为贫穷的身世感到自卑,也曾因漂泊在外感到迷茫。

"麦小登"从小生长在单亲家庭,吃"百家饭"长大。2013年,"麦小登"一家被识别为贫困户,靠着亲戚东拼西凑的2000元钱,她圆了大学梦。毕业后,"麦小登"当过编辑、摆过摊、做过兼职老师、送过外卖。利用学新闻的专业优势,"麦小登"开始尝试拍摄短视频,记录日常生活。

2019年,父亲王云坡病情加重,为了照顾父亲,"麦小登"回到家乡,给父亲买空调、开老式拖拉机收麦子、骑三轮车卖西瓜……"麦小登"尽自己最大的努力守护家庭。

回家,也让"麦小登"的作品获得了"新生"。带着美好的祝愿和增加收入的期待,"麦小登"开始用镜头讲述自己的故事。田间地头、老旧小院,赶集会、收小麦、煮牛肉、蒸馒头……城里人看到真实的农村,农村人看到熟悉的场景,她的粉丝越来越多。

麦小登
Mai Xiaodeng

刚开始,"麦小登"想让父亲出镜,但王云坡接受不了这种"新潮"

and a delivery person. Making use of her professional advantages in journalism, Mai Xiaodeng began to shoot short videos to record her daily life.

In 2019, her father Wang Yunpo became seriously ill. To take care of her father, Mai Xiaodeng returned to her hometown. She bought an air conditioner for her father, drove the old-fashioned tractor to harvest wheat, and rode a tricycle to sell watermelons. Mai Xiaodeng did everything she could to provide for her family.

Home also gave the works of Mai Xiaodeng a new life. With good wishes and expectation of higher income, she began to tell her stories on camera. In her videos appeared the fields, the old yard, the rural fairs, along with harvesting wheat, stewing beef, and steaming buns, and so on. Through her lens city people saw the real countryside, while rural people saw familiar scenes. Her videos gained her a growing number of fans.

Mai Xiaodeng wanted her father Wang Yunpo to appear in the clips, but he could not accept this strange new fashion at first. He finally surrendered and agreed because of his daughter's unceasing entanglement, but he was always ill at ease when facing the lens and chose always to cling to something in his hand to cover his shyness and nervousness. Wang Yunpo's clumsy and unsophisticated appearances won him many fans. He then registered a Tiktok account under the name of Wulaoge (the 5th elder brother). Netizens left comments under the videos of Mai Xiaodeng, "Watching Wulaoge makes me think of my father."

In Mai's videos, there are laughter, tears, displeasure, and anger, but what they always present is hope and courage for life that the father and daughter cherish. Now, they have successfully lifted themselves out of poverty and their life is improving.

Garlic in Niutun Town, Hua County in Henan Province encountered wretched sales in June 2020. Mai Xiaodeng used live broadcasts to help the town's farmers sell garlic on the Internet. It took her just half an hour to make 5,000 sales. She then helped pick the garlic, pack the bales, and send them off to logistics for delivery to buyers. She worked until two or three o'clock the next morning and later recalled "That was a fatiguing day. But I felt happy since I could be of some help."

Thanks to the Internet, Mai Xiaodeng's stories of a new countryside continue.

的方式，架不住女儿的软磨硬泡才同意了，不过，视频中的王云坡习惯手里拿着东西，来掩盖自己的害羞和紧张。王云坡的笨拙与可爱，让他收获了很多粉丝。他自己也注册了一个抖音账号，取名"五老哥"。有网友在"麦小登"的视频下留言，"看到'五老哥'，不禁想起了自己的父亲"。

在"麦小登"的视频里，有笑、有泪、有嗔、有气，但不变的是父女俩对生活的希望和勇气。如今，父女俩已成功脱贫，日子越来越好。

2020年6月，河南省滑县牛屯镇大蒜滞销。得知消息后，"麦小登"在网络上以直播的形式帮助蒜农卖蒜。挑拣大蒜、打包运输，"麦小登"用半个小时卖出5000单大蒜，忙到凌晨两三点。"那一天特别累，但能帮到别人，感到很开心。"

借助互联网的力量，"麦小登"的新田园故事还在继续。

【全景】从灯火辉煌到网路通畅

电网作为经济社会发展的重要基础设施，与人民群众的获得感、幸福感息息相关。

河南加强电网基础设施建设，2016—2018年累计投资306亿元，完成53个贫困县、6492个贫困村、1235个深度贫困村电网脱贫改造。2019—2020年在贫困地区投资111亿元，重点完成贫困县123座变电站建设及1500个非贫困村电网改造。开辟光伏扶贫项目绿色通道，保障全省2万余个光伏扶贫电站及时并网投运，累计全额支付购电费31.2亿元，及时转付新能源补贴8.1亿元，惠及贫困户40.6万户。执行降低用电成本、电费减免等政策，降低了扶贫产业以及贫困户的用电成本。

河南加大对贫困地区网络建设的投入，2016年以来对农村地区网络建设投入资金286.9亿元，引导电信运营公司推出面向贫困户的优惠套餐，省内3.4万所中小学全部实现接入百兆网络。对8000个贫困村、10000户贫困帮扶对象开展电商帮扶，建设电商服务站1217个，开展电

【Panorama】Brilliantly Illuminated Nights and Good Network Connection

The power grid is an important infrastructure for economic and social development, on which people's sense of growth and happiness depend.

Henan Province has reinforced its construction of power grid infrastructure. A total of 30.6 billion *yuan* was invested to upgrade rural power grids in 53 impoverished counties, 6,492 poor villages, and 1,235 villages severely stricken by poverty from 2016 to 2018. 11.1 billion *yuan* was further put into poor areas for the construction of 123 transformer substations in poor counties and for rural grid renovation in 1,500 non-poor villages from 2019 to 2020. A green channel for photovoltaic poverty alleviation projects was opened to ensure that more than 20,000 photovoltaic poverty alleviation power stations in the province were put into operation in a timely manner. A total of 3.12 billion *yuan* was generated from electricity purchases and 810 million *yuan* of new energy subsidies were transferred, benefiting 406,000 poor households. Henan has implemented policies to reduce electricity costs and lower energy bills on power consumption costs for poverty-alleviation industries and poor households.

电力施工
power construction

商培训 3599 场、45117 人次。推广普及信息进村入户和智慧党建、智慧农业等应用，助力数字乡村建设。

14. 环境整治

【故事】赵老屯里的"新故事"

赵胜利是宜阳县香鹿山镇赵老屯村人，20 多年前，他离开了家乡，去了洛阳市打工。那时候，跟赵胜利一起外出打工的赵老屯村年轻人特别多。

赵老屯村坐落在香鹿山上的丘陵沟岔之间，隋唐时期，这里是隐藏深山之间的屯兵之地。全村辖 9 个自然村，共 338 户 1530 人，耕地面积 2885 亩。因为土地瘠薄，沟壑纵横，灌木丛生，长期以来，村民只能靠种几亩粮食糊口。因为穷，赵老屯村逐渐成了人口外流的"空心村"。

赵胜利常年在外打工，每当别人问起家乡，他总是不愿细说。

2018 年，赵老屯村科学编制村庄建设，确定"小青砖、黄土墙、半坡顶、转木门"的传统豫西民居风格并进行整体改造，深挖历史文化，保留老街老院老窑风貌，努力打造乡村旅游集散地。

赵胜利在外打工 20 多年，挣了钱，也在城市里买了房。每年春节，他都会带着老婆孩子回老家，2019 年春节回到老家，赵胜利大吃一惊。平整的柏油路从村口直通各家门口，破败的民房变成一座座古朴的联排新屋，曾经垃圾堆积的角落变成小游园……

2020 年 1 月初，提前回老家的赵胜利看到一拨拨来自洛阳、郑州的游客，开着车子，带着孩子，翻山越岭来到了赵老屯。游客们喜欢到村头路旁花田里，闻闻迷迭香沁人心脾的芳香；喜欢住着老窑洞、老瓦房里，体验一下传统豫西民居的生活；喜欢到村子里的农耕文化馆、花椒展示厅、迷迭香泡脚体验馆，感受赵老屯村的"芳香产业"。

Henan has increased its investment in network construction in the poverty-stricken areas. Since 2016, it has invested 28.69 billion *yuan* in network construction in rural areas, guided telecom operators to launch preferential packages for poor households, and provided all 34,000 primary and secondary schools in the province with 100 MB networks. Henan provided E-commerce assistance to 10,000 poor households in 8,000 poor villages, built 1,217 E-commerce service stations, and conducted 3,599 E-commerce training sessions for 45,117 people. Henan also provided information to villages and households and promoted the use of online applications such as Smart Party Construction and High-tech Agriculture to help with the development of village digitalization.

14. Environment Renovation

【Case】 New Stories in Zhaolaotun Village

Zhao Shengli was born in Zhaolaotun Village, Xianglushan Town, Yiyang County. Over 20 years ago, he left his hometown and went to Luoyang City to work. At that time, many young people from his village preferred to work in the city.

Zhaolaotun Village is located between hills and ravines on the Xianglu Mountain, and served as a troop station hidden among mountains in the Sui and Tang dynasties. The village has jurisdiction over 9 natural villages, a total of 338 households with 1,530 people, and 2,885 *mu* of arable land. The soil was poor, ravines and gullies crisscrossed, and bushes flourished everywhere. For a long time, the villagers could only rely on a few acres of grains to survive. Poverty gradually made Zhaolaotun Village a sparsely-populated village as people began leaving for better opportunities elsewhere.

Zhao Shengli worked outside all year round. Whenever people asked about his hometown, he was always reluctant to say much about it.

In 2018, Zhaolaotun Village started a scientific village construction project and decided the overall construction would be in the traditional western Henan folk house style with small grey bricks, loess walls, sloping roof, and wooden doors. They probed into history and culture, retained the style of the old streets, old courtyards, and old kilns, and made efforts to build a rural tourism hub.

More than 20 years of work in the city was rather rewarding and made

赵老屯
Zhaolaotun Village

因为新冠肺炎疫情,赵胜利在老家住了3个月。这一住,留住了他的心,他决定不回打工的城市了,着手投资在自家小院里办农家饭店。

2020年5月,赵家小院儿开始营业,跟着别人干了20多年的赵胜利,在自己的家乡,开始"烹饪"自己的美好生活。

在赵老屯村,和赵胜利一样,返乡创业的村民还有很多。村民宁旭涛回来了,把自己家二层小楼装修成民宿;常年在外务工的村民张朝伟回来了,在广场边上开了家小卖部;村民宁宏伟把赵老屯的美丽乡村拍成一段段视频,发到网络平台,收到了许多点赞。不少网友询问这是哪里,他都一一回复:我的老家赵老屯。

昔日沟壑纵横、灌木丛生的穷山沟,建设成了功能齐全、错落有致的特色民俗文化休闲地。2021年,赵老屯村130户600多村民吃上了旅游饭,彻底摘掉了贫困的帽子,大步走向全面小康的道路。

Zhao Shengli able to afford an apartment there. However, every Spring Festival, the traditional Chinese New Year, he still took his wife and children back to his hometown. What he saw at the 2019 Spring Festival there amazed him. Smooth asphalt roads led from the entrance of the village to every dwelling. The familiar dilapidated houses were gone and in their places were traditional-style new townhouses. Corners where garbage used to pile up became small gardens.

In early January 2020, Zhao Shengli went back to his hometown ahead of his time schedule and saw flocks of tourists from Zhengzhou City and Luoyang City. These tourists took their families to Zhaolaotun, taking drives a long way up and down the hills. They loved to smell the refreshing fragrance from flower fields by the roadside and the entrance to the village, and to stay in the old caves or tile-roofed houses to experience traditional western Henan life. Tourists also enjoyed the "fragrance industry" of Zhaolaotun in its agricultural culture center, wild pepper exhibition hall, and rosemary foot bath saloon.

Zhao Shengli was quarantined in his hometown for three months during the COVID-19 epidemic. This long stay made him fascinated with his hometown and he decided not to return to the city to work. He instead set about starting an eatery in his own small courtyard.

Zhao's family courtyard business started in May 2020. After working under others for more than 20 years, Zhao Shengli now had his own place in his hometown and expected a promising future.

Many other villagers returned home to start their own businesses as did Zhao Shengli in Zhaolaotun. Villager Ning Xutao came back and furnished his two-story house into a family inn. Absent villager Zhang Chaowei returned and opened a convenience store by the square. Villager Ning Hongwei shoot the beautiful village of Zhaolaotun and posted the series of videos to Internet platforms, receiving many likes. Netizens asked about where it was, and Ning replied respectively, "This is my hometown—Zhaolaotun Village."

The formerly impoverished and inhospitable mountain village with ravines, crisscrossing gullies, and bushes growing everywhere was renovated into a functional, well-designed, leisure resort with traditional folk characteristics. By 2021, more than 600 villagers of 130 households in Zhaolaotun Village were making a living from the new tourism industry. They eliminated poverty and are

【全景】推进贫困地区人居环境整治

人居环境整治是打造生态宜居乡村的基础，也是提升农民生活品质的前提。影响贫困地区人居环境的因素有很多，比如垃圾污水治理、厕所问题、村容村貌等。

河南坚持推进贫困地区人居环境整治。在贫困村开展村庄清洁行动，主要内容是"三清一改"：清理陈年垃圾、清理村内沟塘、清理畜禽粪污等农业生产废弃物，改变影响农村人居环境的不良习惯。2020 年，全省所有行政村生活垃圾基本得到有效治理，农村生活污水治理率达到30%。

林州市庙荒村美丽乡村
A beautiful countryside scene in Miaohuang Village, Linzhou City

"小厕所、大民生"，厕所问题关系到农民生活质量。河南省加大

marching towards a prosperous life in all respects.

【Panorama】 To Improve the Living Conditions in Poor Areas

Improvement to living conditions is the basis of building ecological and livable countryside, and also the first step to improve life quality of farmers. There are many factors that affect living conditions in poor areas such as garbage and sewage treatment, toilets, village appearance, and so on.

Henan has persisted in reinforcing rural living environment improvement initiatives in the impoverished areas. In the impoverished villages, a campaign has been launched to clean up old garbage, ditches and ponds, agricultural wastes such as livestock and poultry dung, and kick bad habits that affect the living environment in rural areas. By 2020, household waste in all administrative villages of the province had been treated effectively and the sewage treatment rate in rural areas had reached 30%.

"A small toilet prominently reflects livelihood." The issue of toilets is about the quality of farmers' lives. Henan increased funding support for toilet improvement in the poverty-stricken areas, allocating 260 million *yuan* in prizes and subsidies from provincial public finance to the impoverished counties, exceeding half of the province's total funds for toilet renovation in 2019. Poor households willing to rebuild the sanitary toilets were given priority with free assistance and a chance to become the model for the whole village. A maintenance service system and a feces collection and utilization system were established after the renovation of toilets. By 2020, 85% of all administrative villages in the province had had access to sanitary toilets.

Once the overall external environment of the village was renovated, the courtyards of the farmers' own homes should also be renovated. Henan Province popularized "the five standards for a beautiful courtyard" in poor areas, carrying out renovations in the yard, water, kitchen, wire, and toilets. Poor households' family environment was greatly improved. Now the yard is clean and tidy, the kitchen is bright and sanitary, and everything is in its place. Places inside and outside the courtyard, in front of and behind the house are all beautified and covered with green, creating a beautiful, neat, sanitary, green, civilized, and harmonious courtyard.

对贫困地区改厕的资金支持力度，2019年省级财政对贫困县的改厕奖补资金达2.6亿元，超过全省改厕奖补资金的一半；对有意愿改建无害化卫生厕所的贫困户，做到优先改、免费改、示范改；抓好改厕之后的管护服务，建立维修服务体系和粪污收集利用体系。2020年，全省行政村卫生厕所普及率达到85%。

村庄整体外部环境改造好了，农民自己家的庭院也要改造好。河南省在贫困地区推进了"五美庭院"建设，开展改院、改水、改厨、改线、改厕等工作，贫困户的家庭环境得到提升，庭院干净整洁，厨房清洁卫生，物品摆放有序，院内院外、房前屋后得到绿化美化，真正成了"整洁美、卫生美、绿化美、文明美、和谐美"的美丽庭院。

15. 消费扶贫

【故事】农产品搭上高速服务区"快车"

今年50多岁的黄根全是济源示范区大峪镇王庄村村民，妻子因为做过手术不能干重活，再加上家里有两个上学的学生，在纳入贫困户之前，家里收入全靠黄根全一个人在附近打零工赚钱。尽管生活艰难，黄根全却一直心怀梦想，希望有朝一日能脱贫致富，过上红红火火的日子。

2015年，河南交通投资集团成为该村的对口帮扶单位，工作队入村不久，就根据黄根全家的情况，建议他扩大种植蟠桃。在纳入贫困户之前，黄根全也曾尝试过种植1亩多的蟠桃，但是由于当时没有技术，没有经验，想大干又不敢干。之后政府出台了各种激励政策，鼓励和引导农户发展产业，扶贫工作队还免费帮他提供果树苗、承诺帮助销售，让他打消顾虑，只管放心地把果树种好。就这样，2016年，黄根全又承包了2亩地种植蟠桃。

2018年6月，黄根全种的蟠桃挂果了，刚好赶上村里举办全市旅游节开幕式的活动，蟠桃很快就被抢购一空。尝到甜头的黄根全把果树面积扩大到六七亩，并增加了油桃品种。

15. Poverty Alleviation through Increasing Consumption

【Case】Agricultural Products Getting Aboard the Express of the Highway Service Area

Huang Genquan, a villager in Dayu Town, Jiyuan Demonstration Area, is in his fifties this year. His wife cannot take on heavy work following a surgery and their two kids are still at school. The whole family lived off what Huang Genquan earned from some part-time jobs in the neighborhood and as a result became registered as an impoverished household. Although life was tough, Huang Genquan always cherished a dream of eliminating poverty for prosperity.

In 2015, the Henan Transport Investment Group was designated as the combined support unit for the village. Shortly after having resided in the village, the work team suggested that Huang expand the planting of flat peaches. Before being registered as a poverty household, Huang Genquan never tried to plant more than one *mu* of flat peaches, but for want of technology and experience, he did not dare plant more. When poverty reduction began, the government introduced various incentive policies to encourage and guide farmers to develop their industries. The poverty alleviation team also provided Huang with fruit saplings for free and promised to help him sell his produce so he could ease his worries and focus on fruit trees. In 2016, Huang undertook another two *mu* of land by contract for planting flat peaches.

In June 2018, Huang Genquan's peach trees yielded fruit. It was just in time for the opening ceremony of the city's tourism festival held in the village. Huang's peaches were soon sold out. Becoming aware of the potential benefits, Huang expanded his orchard to about six or seven *mu* and added nectarine trees.

At the harvest season of 2020, the orchard was full of fruit, but this time Huang was not happy. COVID-19 made selling his produce a big problem. Although the first secretary of their village helped with online sales while retail channels remained open, they did not help much. Huang Genquan was worried, brows knitted. Learning about the plight, the village-based work staff contacted Henan Transport Investment Group just in time. They quickly came to inspect the sample fruits, tasted them, and organized supporting units to carry out "buying products instead of donating money" and "helping via buying" activities.

2020年，又到了收获季节，果园里硕果累累，但黄根全却高兴不起来，由于受新冠疫情的影响，虽然有第一书记线上带货及散客购买等渠道，但仍解决不了大问题，黄根全愁眉不展。驻村队员得知情况后，及时和河南交通投资集团联系对接，看样品、尝味道，组织帮扶单位开展了"以购代捐""以买带帮"等活动。

高速公路服务区的王庄农产品
Agricultural products from WangZhuang Village in the highway service area

还有什么更好的平台帮助销售呢？河南交通投资集团想到了自己系统内的高速公路服务区，那里常年车来车往，人流量大，是个销售产品的好地方。很快，高速公路服务区的超市里尝试开设了扶贫农产品专区，黄根全家的水果摆上了连霍高速郑州北服务区的专柜，因为柜台位置好，打着"产品品质好，又是扶贫农产品"标签，水果很快就卖完了。同时上架的还有位于王庄村的济源大美大峪实业有限公司的扶贫农产品，包括五谷杂粮、土鸡蛋、笨蜂蜜、茶叶等产品，也颇受欢迎，销售良好。截至2020年8月底，12000斤蟠桃、7000斤油桃销售一空，黄根全的脸上又露出了笑容。

这次成功的尝试蹚出了一条新路，省交通运输厅以高速服务区为平

"What better platforms are there to help with the selling?" Henan Transport Investment Group imagined the highway service area within its own system, where cars came and went all year round, facilitating a large flow of people. They decided that it was a good place to sell products. Soon, the service area stores tried a special section for poverty-alleviation agricultural products. The fruits from Huang's family were positioned on the shelves in Zhengzhou North Service Area on Lian-Huo Highway. A preferable position and a publicity stunt of "good qualified poverty alleviation agricultural products" ensured that Huang's fruit was soon sold out. Along with the fruit on the shelf were other poverty alleviation agricultural products from Jiyuan Damei Dayu Industrial Co., LTD., including whole grains, farm eggs, honey, tea, and other items that also sold well. By the end of August, 6,000 kilograms of flat peaches and 3,500 kilograms of nectarines had all been sold out. A smile came back to Huang Genquan's face.

This successful attempt inspired a new approach. The Provincial Department of Transportation took the highway service area as the platform and set up a special display area for well-known or new poverty alleviation agricultural products from the impoverished areas. At the same time, with the help of billboards, electronic screens and other facilities, they succeeded in popularizing the products. Statistics show that the province has set up 290 exhibition areas in 101 pairs of qualified service zones, covering an area of about 2,200 square meters, with a total sales amount of 48,416,000 *yuan* in 2020, and directly providing employment for 370 people in the impoverished areas. Now, this poverty alleviation through consumption model in Henan has spread to the whole country.

【Panorama】 Poverty Alleviation through Consumption Making Farmers' Money Bags Swell

Poverty alleviation through consumption links poverty reduction products, increasing farmers' income, and consumer demands, having a clear bearing on people's lives. Since 2020, Henan Province has taken poverty alleviation through consumption as an important measure to cope with the COVID-19 pandemic and as a crucial means for the decisive battle against poverty, strengthened overall

台，设置消费扶贫农产品专柜、展销专区，代销直销贫困地区名优特新农产品，加大农产品销量，同时，还借助广告牌、电子屏等设施加大宣传，扩大农产品知名度。据统计，全省累计在具备条件的 101 对服务区设立展销专区 290 个，占地面积合计约 2200 平方米，2020 年累计销售金额 4841.6 万元，直接吸纳贫困地区人员就业 370 人。如今，这种消费扶贫的河南模式在全国进行了推广。

【全景】消费扶贫鼓起农民"钱袋子"

消费扶贫一头连着扶贫产品，关系着农户收入；一头连着消费需求，关系着群众生活。2020 年以来，河南省把消费扶贫作为应对新冠肺炎疫情冲击的重要举措，作为决战决胜脱贫攻坚的重要抓手，加强统筹协调、完善政策实施，全力推进消费扶贫。2020 年，全省各层级组织购买和帮助销售贫困地区扶贫产品突破 457 亿元。

加大组织推进力度。河南省委、省政府把消费扶贫作为 2020 年脱贫攻坚重要任务精心谋划部署，制定了《河南省消费扶贫 2020 年工作要点》《河南省消费扶贫六项行动的实施方案》，明确河南省财政厅、商务厅、农业农村厅等 26 家部门责任，落实省辖市、县（区、市）主体责任。把消费扶贫工作纳入各省辖市和济源示范区定点扶贫、"校地结对帮扶"精准扶贫行动、结对帮扶贫困县脱贫攻坚成效考核的重要内容。

构建保障服务机制。帮扶政策支持：河南省财政厅、河南省扶贫办等共同出台推进政府采购贫困地区农副产品的意见，提供政策支持。基础条件支持：截至 2020 年底，全省乡镇快递网点覆盖率达 100%，累计认定 95 个电商进农村综合示范县，实现 53 个贫困县全覆盖，累计建成县级电商扶贫公共服务中心 121 个、乡村电商服务站点 2.35 万个，利用电商促进农产品上行销售 669 亿元。产品品牌支持。编制了全省《扶贫产品名录》，国务院扶贫办共认定河南扶贫产品 20500 个，共涉及 141

planning and coordination, and improved policy implementation to vigorously promote poverty alleviation through consumption. By 2020, the purchase and sale of poverty alleviation products in the impoverished areas organized by the Party and government bodies at all levels in the province exceeded 45.7 billion *yuan*.

First, Henan bolstered Party organization and leadership. Henan provincial Party committee and government took poverty alleviation through consumption as a vital task in 2020, formulated an overarching plan, launched *Key Points of Poverty Alleviation through Consumption in Henan Province in 2020* and *Plan for Implementing Six Measures of Poverty Alleviation through Consumption in Henan Province*. The plans clearly stated the responsibilities of 26 units, including Henan Finance Department, Commerce Department and Department of Agriculture and Rural Affairs, and made sure that provincial cities, counties (including districts) and cities are responsible for implementation. Poverty alleviation through consumption has been included in the evaluation for targeted poverty alleviation in provincial cities and Jiyuan Demonstration Area, and for combined support for targeted poverty alleviation of poor counties.

Second, Henan established a guarantee service mechanism to ensure support. Policy Support: Henan Finance Department and Poverty Alleviation Office jointly issued the opinions on promoting government procurement of agricultural and sideline products from the impoverished areas to provide policy support. Basic Conditions Support: By the end of 2020, the province's township express delivery network coverage had reached 100%, including 53 impoverished counties. A total of 95 demonstration counties with E-commerce in rural areas had been identified. Altogether 121 county-level E-commerce poverty alleviation public service centers and 23,500 rural E-commerce service stations had been built, and 66.9 billion *yuan* of agricultural products had been promoted by E-commerce. Product Brand Support: The provincial Lists of Poverty Alleviation Products was made. Poverty Alleviation Office of the State Council identified 20,500 poverty alleviation products in Henan, involving 6,027 suppliers in 141 counties (or cities or districts). Henan led local governments to establish 4,518 trade markets for poverty alleviation through consumption and identified 3,833 certified agricultural products as poverty alleviation ones. Honors and Rewards Support: In the screening of National and Provincial Poverty Alleviation Awards, and

个县（市、区）、6027个供应商。引导各地建立消费扶贫交易市场4518个，认证贫困县"三品一标"扶贫产品3833个。表彰激励支持。在国家和省级脱贫攻坚奖、"河南省社会扶贫先进集体和先进个人"等评选表彰中，对消费扶贫贡献突出的集体和个人给予倾斜。

设立消费扶贫专区

Special sections for agricultural products under the initiative of poverty alleviation through consumption

扎实推进"三专一平台"。专柜方面，召开专柜企业业务对接会，17个省辖市和济源示范区与国务院扶贫办推荐的11家企业对接，共同制定了专柜建设实施方案，明确了各自专柜的布放任务和完成时间节点。截至2020年底已实际落地专柜2475台，实现数据直连直报917台。专馆方面，省级建成2个消费扶贫生活馆，营业面积超过10000平方米。各地已陆续建设或改造消费扶贫生活专馆355个，实现数据直连直报19个。专区方面，截至2020年底，各地已陆续开设消费扶贫专区1774个，实现数据直连直报5个。其中在高速公路服务区创新性地开展扶贫

Advanced Collectives and Individuals for Poverty Alleviation in Henan Province, those made valuable contributions in poverty alleviation through consumption were put first.

Third, Henan made solid progress in the building of "the three specials and one platform." Counter enterprise business matchmaking meetings were held for special counters. 17 provincial cities and Jiyuan Demonstration Zone were paired with 11 enterprises recommended by the State Council Poverty Alleviation Office. They jointly formulated the implementation plan for counter construction and defined the task and finish time. By the end of 2020, 2,475 counters had been in use, among which 917 counters could provide direct link and report. In terms of poverty alleviation living centers, two provincial living centers had been built with a business area of more than 10,000 square meters. Local governments successively built or renovated 355 special poverty alleviation centers, among which 19 could provide direct link and report. In terms of special zones, 1,774 poverty alleviation zones had been set up in various localities by the end of 2020, among which 5 could provide direct link and report. The creative poverty alleviation initiative carried out in the highway service area established a total of 290 exhibition sections in the 82 pairs of qualified service zones, covering an area of 1,711 square meters. 113,470 items of poverty alleviation agricultural products were displayed and sold, with a total sales amount of about 45.01 million *yuan*. In terms of China's social poverty alleviation network platform, a total of 4,388 poverty alleviation product suppliers have registered on the platform, and 18,228 poverty alleviation products have been displayed on it.

产品消费扶贫行动，累计在具备条件的82对服务区设立展销专区290个，面积达1711平方米，展销扶贫农产品113470件，销售金额约4501万元。中国社会扶贫网平台方面，全省共有4388个扶贫产品供应商入驻中国社会扶贫网平台，18228个扶贫产品在中国社会扶贫网平台上展示。

第三章

全面胜利

Chapter III

A Sweeping Victory

在决战脱贫攻坚、决胜全面小康的征程中，河南始终坚持问题导向，突出重点帮扶、强化薄弱环节，保证全省脱贫攻坚目标如期实现。与此同时，坚持把巩固拓展脱贫成果、防止返贫摆在重要位置，并抓好查漏补缺、巩固提升，以增强脱贫成果的可持续性，确保全省脱贫攻坚最终的质量。

一、聚焦重点难点，攻克最后贫困堡垒

河南省70%以上贫困人口分布在大别山区、伏牛山区、太行山区、黄河滩区，河南把"三山一滩"地区作为脱贫攻坚主战场，先后出台多项措施抓政策落实、项目落地、帮扶措施落细。仅2020年，河南省就向"三山一滩"地区拨付中央、省级财政专项扶贫资金65.98亿元，占全省资金总量的77.33%。对不宜人居的深石山区，在做好自愿易地搬迁的同时，河南省还引导组织群众因地制宜发展产业，确保搬迁之后的群众能就业、有稳定收入。

对卢氏县等4个深度贫困县，每个县倾斜安排专项扶贫资金7000万元，在深度贫困县由省级财政给予一次性补助2000万元，用于设立扶贫小额信贷风险补偿金；将城乡建设用地增减挂钩节余指标跨省域调剂资金全部用于支持深度贫困县发展。针对1235个深度贫困村，省财政为未脱贫村倾斜安排2.7亿元专项扶贫资金；组织动员1173家企业对所有深度贫困村结对帮扶全覆盖。2019年，在继续加大政策、资金等支持之外，组织4个经济实力较强省辖市、4个省直涉农单位结对帮扶4个深度贫困县，深度贫困村驻村第一书记和工作队全部调整为由省、市选派。

"不愁吃、不愁穿、义务教育、基本医疗、住房安全有保障"是贫困人口脱贫的基本标准。针对这些，河南省专门围绕贫困人口稳定实现"两不愁三保障"和饮水安全，开展多项专项行动，巩固基本医疗有保

In the decisive battle against poverty and towards a moderately prosperous society, Henan has always adhered to the problem-oriented approach, highlighted targeted support, and strengthened the weak points to meet poverty alleviation objectives on schedule. At the same time, Henan has insisted that consolidating and expanding the achievements of poverty alleviation and defending against a slide back into poverty be the priority. Henan has done a good job detecting leaks and supplying deficiencies to enhance the sustainability of poverty alleviation success and guarantee the quality of poverty alleviation in the province.

I. Focusing on Key Problems and Overcoming the Last Bulwark of Poverty

More than 70% of the impoverished population in Henan Province live in the Dabie Mountain area, the Funiu Mountain area, the Taihang Mountain area and the Yellow River beach area. Henan has taken the "three mountain areas and one beach area" as its main battlefields for poverty alleviation and introduced measures to ensure the implementation of policies, projects, and metrics. In 2020 alone, Henan allocated central and provincial financial funds of 6.598 billion *yuan* to the impoverished "three mountain areas and one beach area," accounting for 77.33% of the total provincial capital. In inhospitable remote mountain regions, in addition to encouraging voluntary relocation, Henan has guided and organized people to develop industries in accordance with the local conditions, to ensure that the people can find jobs and enjoy a stable income after relocation.

The financial sector allocated 70 million *yuan* as a special poverty alleviation fund for ending poverty in Lushi County and three other deeply impoverished counties, along with a one-time subsidy of 20 million *yuan* from the provincial finance department to establish microloans. Cross-province regulation fund linking surplus cropland quotas with the amount of land used for urban and rural construction has been completely used for boosting deeply impoverished counties. The provincial financial sector allocated 270 million *yuan* of special poverty alleviation funds to those villages still under the poverty line and mobilized 1,173 enterprises to pair with the impoverished villages for assistance. In 2019, in addition to further strengthening policy and financial support, the provincial

障"清零"成果，贫困人口医疗费用合规报销比例稳定在90%左右、大病救治率100%，贫困慢性病患者家庭医生签约率100%；对建档立卡贫困户、低保户、农村分散供养特困人员、贫困残疾人家庭等4类重点对象危房存量逐户排查鉴定和改造；开展水利脱贫攻坚问题清零行动，建档立卡贫困人口饮水安全全部达标。

　　针对无业可就、无业可扶、无力脱贫的贫困老年人、重病患者、重度残疾人等特殊贫困群体，河南全面落实社会保障政策，确保他们在脱贫路上不掉队。2020年，河南省将农村低保标准提高到每人每年不低于4260元，将22%的建档立卡贫困人口纳入低保；农村特困人员基本生活标准提高到年人均不低于5538元，惠及50万人；基础养老金最低标准达到每人每月108元，惠及375.67万建档立卡贫困人口；全面落实残疾人两项补贴，惠及215万人。推进县、乡、村各级福利院、养老院及社会养老机构建设，对失能半失能等人员提供集中托养、日间照料、邻里照护等服务，实现"托养一个人、解放一家人"。

finance sector organized four economically strong provincial cities and four provincial agriculture-related units to pair up with the four deeply impoverished counties. And the village-based first secretaries and work teams to these places were all redesignated by the provincial and municipal Party branches.

"No need to worry about food and clothing, compulsory education, basic medical care, or dilapidated houses" are important benchmarks for removing the poor from poverty. Targeted these objectives, Henan carried out a number of special actions to ensure life stability of the poor population and to realize the "two assurances" and the "three guarantees" along with assuring drinking water safety and guaranteeing basic medical care. Henan achieved a stable reimbursement rate of medical expenses for the poor at around 90%, a serious diseases treatment rate reaching 100%, and the doctor assigning rate to poor patients with chronic diseases reaching 100%. Henan also arranged house-to-house investigations for identification and renovation of the dilapidated houses owned by four kinds of targeted households: households registered as living in poverty, households eligible for subsistence allowances, individuals living in extreme poverty on basic assistance in rural areas, families of people with disabilities affected by poverty Poverty alleviation through water conservancy was also carried out and drinking water safety of all the registered poor people have met standards.

Henan has fully implemented social security policies to ensure special impoverished groups such as poor old people, seriously ill patients and severely disabled people who either are not wanted in any job or have no business to be helped and are thereby unable to lift themselves out of poverty are not left behind. In 2020, Henan raised rural subsistence allowances to no less than 4,260 *yuan* per person per year and 22% registered poor people were covered by the system. The basic living standards of rural people in extreme poverty were raised to no less than 5,538 *yuan* per person per year, benefiting 500,000 people. The minimum basic pension went up to 108 *yuan* per person per month, benefiting 3.7567 million registered poor people. The two subsidies for people with disabilities were fully implemented, benefiting 2.15 million people. Construction of welfare homes, nursing homes and social institutions for the aged at county, town and village

通村公路（南窑村）
Roads to the village (Nanyao Village)

levels is boosted to provide intensive care, day care, neighborhood care and other services to the disabled and semi-disabled people, freeing the whole family by providing for the one person who needs care in the institution.

二、注重作风建设,保障增强扶贫实效

开展专项治理。河南在全省持续开展扶贫领域腐败和作风问题专项治理,重点解决责任落实不到位、工作措施不精准、形式主义等问题。特别是针对个别地方干部思想作风上存在的"松""躁""粗""虚"等问题,严防松劲懈怠等现象发生。建立41个监测点,对基层在脱贫攻坚中存在形式主义、官僚主义问题及时发现和纠正。开展扶贫领域信访问题专项治理,实行领导包案、台账管理等制度,及时妥善解决群众反映的问题。

减轻基层负担。治理扶贫领域困扰基层的突出问题,让基层干部把更多的精力放在为群众办实事上。改进完善调研督导方式,通过暗访或开展调研指导,掌握一手资料、摸清真实情况,帮助基层解决苗头性、倾向性问题;实行年度计划管理,统筹开展督查检查、考核评估等工作,日常督查以暗访、调研和群众举报、信访反映问题核查为主;整合考核内容,把年度集中考核和平时工作情况结合起来,引导各地注重抓好日常工作;精简文件会议,提高文件、会议质量,省级召开的脱贫攻坚会议绝大部分采取视频会议形式;用好全省精准扶贫信息管理平台、扶贫大数据信息系统等,减少基层填表报数,让干部少跑路。

组织干部培训。着眼于解决扶贫干部队伍中存在的理论素养不高、作风建设不实等问题,利用全省各级党校和培训学院等,精选师资、精选阵地、精选学员,组织实施针对扶贫干部的全面精准培训,确保培训不走过场、取得成效。2018—2020年,全省扶贫领域干部教育培训实现常态化、全覆盖,累计培训159万人次。

II. Laying Emphasis on Work Style Construction to Ensure More Tangible Results in Poverty Alleviation

The first is to carry out a special campaign. Henan has consistently carried out a special campaign to tackle corruption and work style problems in poverty alleviation, focusing on solving problems such as incomplete responsibility implementation, imprecise measures, along with formalism, especially sloppiness, fickleness, carelessness, and deceptiveness in ideology of some individual local officials. Forty-one monitoring stations have been set up to promptly identify and rectify the problems of formalism and bureaucratism in poverty alleviation at the primary level. A special campaign has been launched to address complaints about poverty alleviation. Additionally, a system was introduced in which leaders assume full responsibility for certain cases and a management standing book was required to solve problems reported by the public promptly and properly.

The second is to lighten burdens on officials at the primary level. Henan addressed salient problems plaguing the primary level officials, allowing them to concentrate on doing practical things for people, as well as improved the inspection and supervision method to grasp first-hand information and to find out the real situation through secret enquiry or conducting research guidance so that they could help the primary level officials nip problems in bud. We implemented annual planning management, and coordinated supervision, inspection, assessment and evaluation. Daily inspections mainly focused on secret inquiries, investigations, reports from the masses, as well as complaints through letters and visits. We integrated the contents of the assessment, combined the annual assessment with the regular work, and guided local governments to focus on their daily work. We made efforts to streamline documents and meetings and to improve the quality of them, which, as a result, led most of the poverty alleviation meetings held at the provincial level to be in the form of video conferences. We made good use of the provincial targeted poverty alleviation information management platform and poverty alleviation big data system to reduce the number of forms meant to be filled out by primary level officials and to spare officials unnecessary errands.

科技特派员郭奎英传授育苗技术
Guo Kuiying, a science and technology commissioner, is teaching villagers how to grow seedlings.

The third is to organize official trainings. Focusing on solving the problems of low theoretical attainment and unreliable work style construction among poverty alleviation officials, Henan made use of Party schools and training colleges at all levels in the province, selected teachers, positions, and trainees, and organized and implemented comprehensive and precise trainings for poverty alleviation officials to ensure that the trainings were effective. During the span between 2018 and 2020, cadre education and training in the field of poverty alleviation in the whole province was normalized, and achieved full coverage with a total of 1.59 million people trained.

三、健全长效机制，巩固拓展脱贫成效

贫困具有多维性、动态性和成因复杂性等特征，一步脱贫易，稳定脱贫难。脱贫后如何巩固脱贫成果，防止返贫，需要兼顾当前和长远利益，协调各方行动，统一规划，整体布局，建立起稳定脱贫长效机制。

健全防止返贫动态监测和帮扶机制。加强监测预警，对脱贫不稳定户、边缘易致贫户等人群，开展常态化监测预警，做到及时发现、快速响应、动态清零。抓好精准帮扶，对有劳动能力的低收入人口，及时落实好产业、就业等帮扶发展的措施，帮助提高内生发展能力；对没有劳动能力的低收入人口，由民政等部门负责进行兜底保障，并逐步提高保障水平。

巩固"两不愁三保障"成果。教育保障方面，要继续实施家庭经济困难学生资助政策，持续抓好控辍保学。医疗保障方面，要认真落实分类资助参保政策，积极做好脱贫人口参保动员工作，优化疾病分类救治措施。住房保障方面，对新出现的危房及时进行鉴定和改造，采取有效形式落实好住房救助政策，切实保障基本住房安全。饮水安全方面，要巩固维护现有农村饮水安全工程成果，不断提升农村供水保障能力。

促进脱贫人口稳定就业。2020年全省建档立卡脱贫户中有287.73万人外出务工，占比43.66%；全省脱贫户年人均工资性收入8983.01元，占年人均纯收入的68.91%。要持续加强技能培训。开展职业教育、农业实用技术等培训，增强脱贫劳动力稳定就业能力。要加大有组织的劳务输出力度，输出地要做好脱贫劳动力组织发动、劳务输出工作。要积极拓宽就近就地就业渠道。灵活采取龙头企业带动、扶贫车间吸纳、公益岗位安置等形式，促进弱劳力、半劳力就近就地就业。加强扶贫车间规范管理，依法合规运营，完善支持政策，确保其充分发挥作用。要大力支持返乡创业，带动脱贫人口就业。

III. Improving Long-term Mechanism to Consolidate and Broaden Our Success in Poverty Alleviation

Poverty is multi-dimensional and dynamic. It is always the result of complex causes. It is easier to abolish poverty than maintain success of the fight. To consolidate our success in poverty alleviation and prevent backsliding into poverty, we should take into account both present gains and long-term benefits, coordinate actions of all parties, make overarching planning and overall layout, and establish a stable long-term mechanism for poverty alleviation.

First, to improve the dynamic monitoring and assistance mechanism to prevent backsliding into poverty. Henan strengthened its disaster monitoring and early warning systems. We carried out regular monitoring and early warning measures for those vulnerable to poverty to ensure timely identification, rapid response, and prompt eradication of potential issues. We will make great efforts in targeted assistance. For the low-income people who are able to work, we will promptly implement support measures to boost industrial development and employment, and help them improve their development capacity all on their own. For the low-income people without the ability to work, civil affairs departments and other administrative ones will make sure of a minimum guarantee in place and an ever-rising guarantee level.

Second, to consolidate the achievements of the "two assurances" and "three guarantees." To ensure education, we should continue to implement the policy of providing financial aid to students from poor families and of enabling school dropouts to get back to school. In terms of medical care, we should conscientiously implement the policy of classified medical subsidies, actively mobilize people out of poverty to participate in medical insurance, and optimize measures for classifying treatment of diseases. For housing security, we should timely identify and renovate emerging dilapidated houses, effectively implement housing assistance policies, and effectively guarantee basic housing safety. To guarantee drinking water safety, we need to consolidate and maintain the existing achievements of rural drinking water safety projects and constantly improve guarantee capacity in the field of rural water supply.

支持脱贫地区乡村特色产业发展壮大。要注重产业后续长期培育。加强脱贫地区产业发展基础设施建设，组织实施特色种养业提升行动，继续实施"田园增收、养殖富民、乡村旅游等"产业发展十大行动，推进特色产业不断发展壮大。要完善全产业链支持措施。加大财政、金融、税收等政策支持，健全生产、加工、仓储保鲜、冷链物流等全产业链，加大科技服务、人才培养等支持力度，广泛开展农产品产销对接活动，深化拓展消费帮扶，提高产业抗风险能力。要强化主体培育和利益联结。大力扶持龙头企业、农民专业合作社和家庭农场，促进其高质量发展。将扶持政策与联动带农效果挂钩，完善利益联结机制，更好更多地带动脱贫户稳定增收、逐步致富。

另外，要做好易地扶贫搬迁后续扶持、扶贫项目资产管理和监督、志智双扶等相关工作。

Third, to facilitate stable employment for people lifted out of poverty. In 2020, 2.8773 million people of the registered households lifted out of poverty in the province went out for non-farming jobs, accounting for 43.66% overall, and the annual per capita wage income of the households lifted out of poverty in the province was 8,983.01 *yuan*, accounting for 68.91% of the annual per capita net income. We should continue to strengthen skills training, carry out vocational education and training in practical agricultural techniques, and enhance the ability of the people lifted out of poverty to find stable jobs. We should increase organized labor output on the premise that the export places do a good job in organizing and mobilizing the labor force already out of poverty. We should actively expand local employment channels, flexibly adopting the measures of mobilization from the leading enterprises and taking-in from poverty alleviation workshops, and of creating welfare work posts, so as to encourage weak labors and semi-able-bodied labors to find local employments. We should enhance standardized management of poverty alleviation workshops, operate in accordance with laws and regulations, perfect supporting policies, and ensure that they play their full roles. We should give strong support to those who return to their hometowns to start businesses and create jobs for people already freed from poverty.

Fourth, to support the development and expansion of rural industries in poverty alleviation areas. We should focus on the follow-up long-term development of industries, reinforce infrastructure construction for industrial development in poverty-stricken areas, organize and implement initiatives to improve featured cultivation and breeding industries, and continue to implement the ten initiatives to develop rural industries such as "income increasing through planting, getting rich through stockbreeding and rural tourism" to develop and strengthen industries with distinctive features. We should perfect the whole industrial chain support measures, increase fiscal, financial and taxation policy support, improve the whole industrial chain of production, processing, warehousing, preservation, cold chain logistics, etc., increase support for technology services and personnel training, extensively conduct activities to link production with marketing of agricultural products, deepen and expand support through consumption, and make industries more resilient to risks. We should

第三章 全面胜利

凉水坪新村群众在跳广场舞（摄影：马秀华）
Villagers of Liangshuiping Village are dancing on the square. (Photographer: Ma Xiuhua)

strengthen the connection between cultivation and benefits, vigorously support leading enterprises, farmers professional cooperatives and family farms to promote high-quality development, link support policies with the effects of pairing-up assistance, improve benefit coupling mechanism, and better incentivize people to escape poverty by steadily increasing their income and marching towards prosperity.

In addition, it is necessary to provide support in the wake of poverty alleviation through relocation, poverty-alleviation projects funds management and supervision, along with motivation and education that relate to poverty alleviation.

四、做好有效衔接，全面推进乡村振兴

乡村振兴是实现中华民族伟大复兴的一项重大任务。全面实施乡村振兴战略的深度、广度、难度都不亚于脱贫攻坚，要完善政策体系、工作体系、制度体系，以更有力的举措、汇聚更强大的力量，加快农业农村现代化步伐，促进农业高质高效、乡村宜居宜业、农民富裕富足。

在脱贫攻坚与实施乡村振兴战略的历史交汇期，要坚持把巩固拓展脱贫攻坚成果放在突出位置，统筹做好同乡村振兴在领导体制、工作体系、发展规划、政策举措、考核机制等方面的有效衔接，从解决建档立卡贫困人口"两不愁三保障"为重点转向实现乡村产业兴旺、生态宜居、乡风文明、治理有效、生活富裕，从集中资源支持脱贫攻坚转向巩固拓展脱贫攻坚成果和全面推进乡村振兴，用乡村振兴巩固拓展脱贫攻坚成果，推动脱贫地区实现更宽领域、更高层次的发展。确定卢氏、嵩县、台前、淅川4个原省定深度贫困县为乡村振兴重点帮扶县，支持各地自主选择巩固拓展脱贫攻坚成果和乡村振兴任务较重的乡镇、村作为重点帮扶对象，增强其巩固脱贫成果及内生发展动力。

推动脱贫攻坚工作体系全面转向乡村振兴。要保持主要帮扶政策总体稳定。在新政策出台实施前，原有政策一律不能退、力度不能减，继续执行到位。过渡期内，在财政政策上，各级要保持财政专项帮扶资金规模不减少，过渡期前3年脱贫县继续实行涉农资金统筹整合试点政策，现有财政相关转移支付继续倾斜支持脱贫地区；在金融政策上，"5万元以下、3年期以内、免担保免抵押、财政贴息"的小额信贷政策继续实行，现有再贷款帮扶政策在展期期间保持不变，加大精准支持企业贷款力度；在土地政策上，专项安排脱贫县年度新增建设用地计划指标，将脱贫地区城乡建设用地增减挂钩节余指标优先在省内公开交易，所得收益主要用于巩固脱贫攻坚成果和推进乡村振兴；在人才政策上，继续

IV. Making Effective Connection and Promoting Rural Revitalization in All Respects

Rural revitalization is a significant task in realizing the great rejuvenation of the Chinese nation. The comprehensive implementation of the rural revitalization strategy is as difficult in both depth and breadth as poverty alleviation. We need to improve our policies, work systems and institutional systems, and take more effective measures to gather stronger forces to accelerate the modernization of agriculture and rural areas, so that agriculture can maintain high-quality and efficient development, rural areas are hospitable and favorable to businesses, and farmers' lives are more prosperous.

In the historical convergence period between poverty alleviation and the implementation of rural revitalization strategies, we must give high priority to consolidating and broadening our success in poverty alleviation, and make an overarching plan for smoothly transferring to rural revitalization in fields of leadership system, work system, development plans, policies, measures and evaluation mechanisms. The focus will shift from addressing the "two assurances" and "three guarantees" for the registered poor population to realizing prosperity of rural industries, ecological friendliness, rural civilization, effective governance, and prosperous life, from gathering resources for poverty alleviation to consolidating and broadening the achievements made in poverty alleviation and comprehensively promoting rural revitalization, so as to promote the development of areas out of poverty to a wider range of fields and a higher level. We should designate the former four deeply impoverished counties: Lushi County, Songxian County, Taiqian County and Xichuan County as the counties with desperate demands for support in rural revitalization. We need to encourage local governments to independently select towns and villages that have the toughest way forward by consolidating our success in poverty alleviation and rural revitalization as the ones that need most support, to consolidate their success in poverty alleviation and to stimulate their internal momentum to develop.

To shift the work of poverty alleviation to rural revitalization, we need to maintain the overall stability of major assistance policies. Before new policies are

实施农村义务教育阶段教师特岗计划、中小学幼儿园教师国家级培训计划、全科医生特岗计划、脱贫地区人才支持计划，深入推行科技特派员制度。要做好帮扶政策衔接。要把国家出台的新政策承接好，立足实际抓好落实，同时要及时对本地本部门出台的原有帮扶政策进行全面梳理，根据中央精神做好优化调整。要合理把握政策调整的节奏、力度和时限，逐步实现由集中资源支持脱贫攻坚向全面推进乡村振兴平稳过渡，确保不影响巩固拓展脱贫攻坚成果。

健全农村低收入人口常态化帮扶机制。在河南省脱贫户中，2020年人均纯收入6000元以下的有8510户，其中丧失和无劳动力占比过半，这类人员很容易滑到贫困线以下；2020年底有脱贫不稳定户3.6万户12万人，返贫风险主要集中在因大病、因残、因就业不稳定，三项合计占比68.8%，这类人员脱贫基础比较脆弱；纳入民政兜底保障的266.7万人、占40%，这类人员对兜底保障政策依赖性比较强。从边缘易致贫户看，全省总规模约5.4万户16.7万人，其中有不少户家底薄，抗风险能力弱，很容易陷入贫困。因此，对上述人员要继续开展动态监测，实行分层分类帮扶。对有劳动能力的，有针对性地支持他们发展产业、转移就业、自主创业；对没有劳动能力的，有针对性地落实好低保、特困人员救助供养、临时救助、医疗保障、养老保障、残疾人救助等政策，做到应保尽保、应兜尽兜。

introduced, the existing policies should not be reduced in intensity and should be fully implemented. During the transition period, in terms of fiscal policies, governments at all levels should keep the scale of special financial assistance funds unchanged. During the first three years of the transition, counties that have been lifted out of poverty should continue to implement the pilot policy of overall planning and integration of agriculture-related funds, and the existing fiscal transfer payments should continue to favor areas that have been lifted out of poverty. In terms of financial policies, we will continue to offer guarantee for mortgage-free microloans less than 50,000 *yuan* in no more than three years with fiscal discount interest, and the existing reloaning assistance policy will remain unchanged during the roll-over period with more targeted support for enterprise loans. For land policies, we should specially arrange indicators of annual newly-increased construction land, carry out the initiative of transferring surplus land quotas in areas out of poverty for urban and rural construction within the province first, and use the earnings mainly to consolidate the success in poverty alleviation and to promote rural revitalization. In terms of personnel policies, we should continue to implement the special post program for teachers in rural areas in compulsory education, the national training programs for teachers in primary and secondary schools and kindergartens, a special post program for general medical practitioners, a talent support program for areas that have already been lifted out of poverty, and further implement sci-tech special commissioner system. We need to join existing policies smoothly with new ones introduced by the state and implement them based the actual situations on the ground. At the same time, we need to comprehensively review the existing policies on assistance issued by local bodies in a timely manner and optimize and adjust them in accordance with central government guidelines. We need to properly control the pace, intensity and time frame of policy adjustments, gradually realize a smooth transition from poverty alleviation with concentrated resources to comprehensively promote rural revitalization, and ensure that our successes in poverty alleviation are not jeopardized.

We should improve the mechanism for regularly supporting low-income people in rural areas. In Henan Province, households out of poverty with a per capita net income under 6,000 *yuan* numbered 8,510 in 2020, among whom

第三章 全面胜利

家园——镇平县七里庄村新貌
Homeland—new look of Qilizhuang Village, Zhenping County

more than half lost or were deprived of labor ability, and thus tended to slip back to poverty. By the end of 2020, there were 36,000 households with 120,000 people who had been lifted out of poverty with the risk of backsliding. The risks of slipping back into poverty were mainly caused by serious diseases, disability, and unstable employment, jointly accounting for 68.8%. These people had a relatively weak foundation for complete poverty alleviation. 2.667 million people had been included in the civil administration bottommost guarantee, accounting for 40% of the total. Such people had strong dependence on the bottommost guarantee policy. As for households tending to fall into poverty, there were about 54,000 households with a total of 167,000 people who were prone to poverty in the province, among which many households were poor and weak in risk resistance, and thus tended to slip back into poverty after having been lifted out of it. Therefore, we should keep on dynamically monitoring the above-mentioned people, and implementing hierarchical and classified assistance. For those who can work, we need to offer targeted support for developing business they are in, for transferring employment, and for self-employment. For those who are deprived of the ability to work, we will carry out targeted policies such as basic living allowances and support to people in extreme poverty with temporary assistance, medical care, old-age pension, and assistance to people with disabilities.